Barnes

A
MEANDER
IN TIME

Mary Grimwade

Produced in Great Britain by Dynamic Impressions Ltd
Design Toni Marshall
Special thanks to David and Susan Boyd, Maisie Brown, Jeanne Dunsford, John Grayson and Marie and Mike Smith

Cover detail – sundial from St Mary's, Barnes

ISBN 0-9542038-1-X

Foreword

The following articles on Barnes were first published as single items in the quarterly Newsletter of the Barnes and Mortlake History Society during the period 1972-2002. Gathered into one volume, they represent many years of research by a dedicated local historian, founder member and Vice-President of the Society; my friend and colleague, Mary Grimwade. They cover many aspects of the history of Barnes, together with personal recollections of everyday village life in both peace and war. Above all, they are a testimony to their author's deep and abiding affection for the place where she was born and where she lived for many years before moving to her present home in East Sheen in 1966.

Mary's parents came to live in Barnes immediately after their honeymoon in 1907 and were the first occupants of No. 8 Kitson Road, newly built on part of the St Mary's Rectory grounds. Their daughter Mary was born in the house shortly before the outbreak of World War I. It was there that she grew up alongside her two brothers, completing the major part of her education at St. Paul's Girls' School before entering Teacher Training College and eventually beginning her professional life as a teacher of History and English.

I first met Mary soon after joining the History Society in 1976. Still feeling a relative newcomer to Barnes, in spite of having lived there for 10 years, it was for me a delight to hear her recall the Barnes she had known as a child. How the market gardens at Walnut Tree Farm were visible from an upper window in Kitson Road, before the row of houses on the north side of Melville Road were completed. Of childhood excursions to fish at the tadpole pool on Barnes Common and how, when her mother went shopping, she always remembered to take a lump of sugar for the Rector's horse, grazing in the Rectory paddock where 99 Church Road now stands. I also learned that the placing of the Edward VII letter box at the junction of Melville and Kitson Roads resulted from her father's urgent request to the Post Office for a box nearer to home than the one in Church Road. It was, however, only when I began my own first ventures into local history research that I learned to appreciate fully the depth of Mary's knowledge of Barnes and its history and her delight in passing this knowledge on to others.

Since those early days we have often worked together, proof-reading and generally preparing many of the History Society's publications for the printers, usually sitting at Mary's dining table. Far from being time spent on dull but necessary chores, invariably these have been happy and often hilarious occasions, in spite of the threat of looming deadlines. Successive editors of the Barnes and Mortlake History Society's Newsletter, including for a time myself, have long appreciated the informative, carefully researched, eminently readable and often highly amusing articles submitted for publication by Mary Grimwade, knowing their popularity with the membership. It gives me great pleasure to know that they are now available to a far wider public.

Maisie Brown,

Vice-President and former Chairman, Barnes and Mortlake History Society.

AVENUE & CEMETERY, BARNES COMMON

15

Mary Grimwade recalls garden fêtes and such-like held in the Asling's garden in Castelnau. She remembers the two daughters in particular and after the family moved to Exeter her parents continued to correspond for some years with the daughters after the death of their parents.

[signature] 17.8.84

NOT·FOR·OURSELVES·ALONE

Contents

First & Second Wartime Life
Childhood Memories of Barnes in the Great War   7
Christmastide in World War Two   9
Wartime Schooling 1939-1940   12

Peace time emergencies
Fire...Fire!   15
The great fire at Barn Elms Farm   17
A Christmas Hero   18
The Great Barnes Flood   19

Barnes Terrace
The Papendiek Family in Barnes   21
Nurserymen and artists   23
Riverside Delights   24
Another boat race of long ago   25

Lesser Barnes authors
Little-known Barnes writers   27
Joseph Comyns Carr   28
A prolific writer   29
Horse dealing in Barnes   30

Local Eccentrics
An Eccentric Barnes Farmer   31
Old Parr   32
Old Reuben   33
Hermitage Cottage and Monk Lewis   34
The Arab boy   35
Philip de Waal   35

Continued

Parish and people

1889 – and all that   37
A Kindly Act   38
The Bad Old Days   39
Vivat Regina – 1897   40
Memories of Essex House   42
Barnes and Mortlake en Fete   44
Not For Ourselves Alone   46
Missing items of Barnes Church Plate   48

Barnes flora

Elizabethan Plantsmen   49
The Elms of Barnes Churchyard   50
The Lobjoits – Market Gardeners of Barnes   51
Wild Flowers   52
The Acacia Man   52

Local gossip

A Minor Scandal   53
Ghoulies and Ghosties   54
Mumming in Barnes   55

Barnes memories

Water Rat Cottage   57
Childhood Memories   57
Sir Arthur Bliss   58
Calling All Parents   59
Bus Journeys from Barnes to Hammersmith   60

Let us now praise famous men

The Lowther family's Suffolk home   63
A Distinguished Friendship   64
Old Nassaurians   65

Map index on fold-out   Back cover
Information on our Historical Society

First & Second Wartime Life

Childhood Memories of Barnes in the Great War 1914-1918

I was born in Kitson Road, Barnes, just before the outbreak of World War One. At first, I imagine, life for most local people went on much as usual, in the firm belief that hostilities would be over by Christmas. My parents kept a maid, who stayed for the first year or so and I have photographs of her pushing my pram, before she left for war work. In the summer of 1916, my brother and I were taken on holiday to Littlehampton, so it was still possible to visit seaside resorts.

I have vague memories of soldiers billeted on us. They were recruits training in the neighborhood, and householders were obliged to take them if they had a spare bedroom. After my father was called up in 1917, my mother was not sent any more troops, as she was a lone woman in the house, but I do recall a woman lodger – perhaps there for company.

In 1918 air raids began at night, and we sheltered in the cellar. A piece of shrapnel broke one of our front windows, and a couple were killed on Barnes Common, so my mother decided to take us to Hadleigh in Suffolk. This was my father's home: for a while we stayed with my grandfather and then spent the spring and summer in lodgings.

Mary aged 2 on holiday at Littlehampton, August 1916

Each morning German prisoners-of-war passed our sitting room window on their way to work on farms. One of them usually rode a cart horse and my brother and I thought he put us in mind of our father and we often smiled as he passed. In return he acknowledged us and my mother said that perhaps he had children of his own at home and we helped to brighten his day.

I recollect being taken one summer's day to a lovely garden in George Street and sitting with other ladies pulling the petals off marigolds. These were thrown into a large galvanised bath, partly filled with water and left to soak. I was told this was "to help wounded soldiers". I have since found there is some therapeutic cure made from this blossom which can help heal cuts and burns.

We returned to Barnes in the late summer of 1918 as it was realised that hostilities were ending. On the morning of November 11 my father was on leave from the Royal Naval Air Service (he served with ground forces at Dunkirk) and I was with him sweeping up autumn leaves in the garden. Suddenly at 11am maroons sounded from Hyde Park and the war was over, but unfortunately my father could not be immediately demobilised and had to return to France for the very cold winter of early 1919.

The 'flu epidemic of that year caused the deaths of hundreds of civilians and my mother later related how every time she went shopping funerals passed along Barnes High Street. I realised years afterwards how frightened she had been of falling ill with two small children to look after but we survived to greet my father when he returned home for good in February 1919.

For many years afterwards one was aware of the aftermath of war, especially in the surrounding area. Queen Mary's Hospital in Roehampton Lane became famous for its work in supplying and fitting artificial limbs and men in blue hospital uniform, usually on crutches, were to be seen sitting on the innumerable seats along the Lane and Barnes Common with the notice on the back "for wounded soldiers". I think they did well with gifts of sweets and cigarettes from passers-by. Then, too, the gracious Star & Garter Home[1] was built on Richmond Hill a further constant reminder of the long term results of the 1914-1918 war.

For me, a wartime child, a new world opened in 1919. A seaside holiday in August preceded beginning school in September and a pattern of peacetime life evolved which I was to enjoy for many years.

Printed September 2002/Newsletter number 162

I recollect being taken one summer's day to a lovely garden in George Street and sitting with other ladies pulling the petals off marigolds. These were thrown into a large galvanised bath, partly filled with water and left to soak. I was told this was "to help wounded soldiers"

[1] Star & Garter Home – built 1924

Christmastide in World War Two

Diary Extracts describing Barnes 65 years ago

29 Nov. 1940   Very cold and the gas pressure low. The day was uneventful but the evening was not. The air raid warning sounded soon after six and it was a dreadful evening. At 7.30 incendiary bombs fell all around us. One in the garden of 2 Kitson Road, others on 15, an empty house, in the road and in the back garden of a house in Melville Road. Everyone rushed out and we handed out our bucket of sand, but the stirrup pump was not needed. The place was like daylight and while the incendiaries were blazing three high explosive bombs fell nearby. We heard more bombs during the evening and the planes never seemed to go away.

30 Nov.   Everyone we saw while out shopping appeared very worried about last night's raid.

1 Dec.   After lunch we walked round Barnes and saw bomb damage from Friday night's raid. A warning sounded just before 10pm. There was a terrific explosion at midnight which woke me. Bombs somewhere near and then there was heavy gunfire, but I soon went off to sleep again. My brother never woke, just groaned!

2 Dec.   No alerts all day.

3 Dec.   During the evening a friend called. His wife and three little girls are in the country and he usually sleeps under the air shaft at Holborn Station. He does A.R.P. work in Holborn twice a week in a stretcher party. He is trying to improve the minds of his fellow A.R.P.[1] workers and reads Henry V with them to prevent them from gambling. About ten, in the black-out and a raid warning, he rode away on a bicycle to spend the night with some other friends.

4 Dec.   My Mother and I went round to friends In Ferry Road for tea. I have not been round there lately. It is now very much tidied up, the road repaired and damaged houses have been pulled down. They are better down than shattered but they leave dreary gaps. Our friends' house has been badly damaged. They have claimed £120 damage, not including roof repairs which the Council has carried out. (This was quite a considerable sum in 1940). The front bedrooms, hall and dining room are more or less unusable and all the front windows are boarded up.

5 Dec.   Probably due to some diet deficiency I have very bad chilblains on my hands and feet. They are so painful I cannot knit and writing is difficult.

8 Dec.   In the afternoon went to Richmond and saw the damage there. Bartons, the drapery store, opposite the station, is completely burnt out and the Library roof has been burnt as well. The Town Hall, Goslings furnishing shop and Ellis, the wine merchants, have also been gutted by fire while up the Hill there have been many high explosive bombs. Walked home through the Park and saw many bomb craters and scores of marks left by incendiary bombs. There must have been hundreds dropped in the Park altogether, went up close to the A.A. guns.[2] There are eight just inside Sheen Gate. The air raid warning sounded at half past five and we had a very bad raid. Fire was reflected in the sky, even up till half past eleven it was still glowing. The raid continued all night and the All Clear did not sound until seven o'clock the next morning.

[1] A.R.P. – Air Raid Precautions
[2] A.A. – Anti-Aircraft guns, commonly known as "Ack-Ack", as this was how they sounded.

Thank goodness. Hitler did not come tonight.

9 Dec.   Everyone full of last night's raid which was admittedly one of the worst on London. Was glad to have a peaceful evening. A very uneventful day.

10 Dec.   Thank goodness. Hitler did not come tonight.

21 Dec.   Last night's raid was directed towards Liverpool but the planes seemed to come over London a great deal.

23 Dec.   In the afternoon went up to Kensington to buy some more presents. The shops are obliged to close at 4.00pm so I did not have long. It snowed during the evening. Listened to the Prime Minister speaking to the Italians.

24 Dec.   The papers call it the "Christmas under Fire" and I suppose it really is, and yet one forgets about the fire and thinks about Christmas. Called on the Rev F.I. Harrison, the Chaplain of Hickey's Almshouses in Sheen Road, Richmond. He showed us his house which is uninhabitable, suffering from the blast of two land mines. I have never seen a house in such a wreck. The furniture is more or less useless, ceilings down, all the doors wrenched off their hinges, windows broken, window frames out, plaster down in all the rooms, banisters out etc.

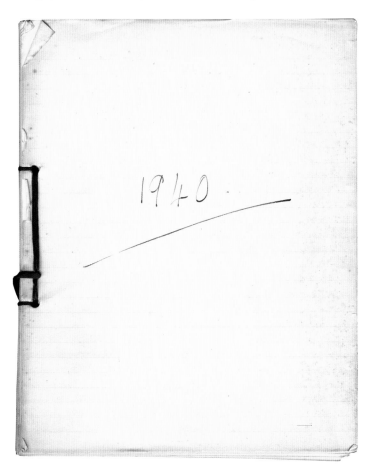

Mary's Diary from 1940

There were no air raid warnings. It was marvellous.

25 Dec. – Christmas Day 1940. To church at St Mary's at 7.30am. The Lady Chapel was used, as the church is not blacked out, but even so I imagine the black out regulations must have been broken. There were no curtains whatever and so the only lights were in the chancel itself and the congregation sat in darkness. We went well up to the front and so we were all right. Our Christmas dinner this year was not turkey, but roast beef instead. Perhaps even more English. However, we had mince pies and Christmas pudding and a bottle of 1919 wine. Good for a war time dinner. We listened in after to the King's speech and then had a walk along the towpath. Home to tea and cut the Christmas cake and then spent a quiet evening peacefully by the fire being lazy and listening to the radio. The air raid warning sirens did not sound, so "Christmas under Fire" was much more peaceful than we imagined.

26 Dec.   There were no warnings for the third night running.

27 Dec.   Rather a bad raid but no bombs in Barnes.

29 Dec.   A very bad raid indeed. The sky was brilliantly alight with the glow of fires and it was obviously London that was on fire. The gunfire was very heavy and we could also hear our fighters up overhead. Eventually the All Clear sounded at half past eleven but when I looked out later the light in the sky seemed even brighter.

30 Dec.   Heard a good many rumours this morning concerning last night's raid on London. I met a friend as I went out shopping and she told me that Victoria Station was damaged and later from another I was told that Liverpool Street Station was still on fire. However, I thought most of this was probably rumour and without any proper qualification. My Mother tried to telephone my Father in the City but the exchange was not working and so we could not find out whether his premises in Cheapside were still standing or not. In the early evening, Father came home and told us about the City fire. His premises are still standing but an absolute island site. The GPO and Telegraph office have gone, six famous city churches, including St. Lawrence Jewry and St. Bride's, Fleet Street, The Guildhall, St. Paul's Chapter House, etc. Streets laid waste and smoke over everything. At present no-one quite knows what is left and what has gone and many buildings now standing will have to be pulled down because they are dangerous. All day fires were still breaking out and firemen were standing by. A nightmare day and night for London citizens. The Lord Mayor spent the night among the firemen and the Prime Minister (Winston Churchill) walked down Cheapside in the afternoon.

31 Dec.   After lunch I had a walk across the Common and went into the Cemetery[3] to behold a tombstone put up to Francis Turner Palgrave, compiler of the Golden Treasury. No warnings this evening and so the Old Year passed out and I hope 1941 will prove far better for us all.

Printed December 1990/Newsletter number 115

floor and so The Old Year passed out and I hope 1941 will prove far better for us all.

---

[3] The Cemetery on Barnes Common, now disused.

Wartime Schooling 1939-1940
At East Sheen Primary, Westfields and Lowther junior mixed and infants schools

In 1992 two classes at the East Sheen Primary School in the Upper Richmond Road have been researching into Second World War events in their locality and I was recently asked to give my personal reminiscences of life at that time. I found great interest and enthusiasm among the pupils.

In return, the Society has been given a photo-copy of extracts from the school logbook for 1939 and 1940 and the following account has been compiled using that original source.

On 3 September 1939 the school staff, recalled from their summer holidays, set in motion plans for the evacuation of those children whose parents wished them moved out of the area. They assembled at the school at 8.30am and then walked to Barnes station to board a train for Windsor due to leave at 11.25am. As it left the station the first air raid warning of the war sounded. The school then closed until further notice. A month later a staff meeting was held at the school, with the divisional officer present, to discuss future arrangements for the education of the many children who had either returned home or not gone away in the first place. Plans went rapidly ahead for on 3 October the school reopened on a two shift system.

Six rooms were made available and from 8.30am to 12 noon girls from Mortlake and Barnes Central Schools were admitted and from 1.30 to 4.30pm boys from the equivalent schools. These times were reversed every fortnight. Two other rooms were allotted to the juniors, 8-10 years old. These pupils came from Mortlake Junior Mixed and Infants and the two church schools, Church of England and Roman Catholic. They were obliged to use the rooms alternately morning and afternoon with East Sheen, Westfields and Lowther Junior Mixed and Infants schools. On the first day 36 children were admitted, but numbers increased rapidly and two weeks later there were 100 on the register, with a further 50 applicants who could not be admitted owing to lack of space.

Gradually difficulties were resolved and by May 1940 the number on the roll was 400. This was undoubtedly due to the fact that the expected aerial attacks had not materialised. However, by June there was fear of invasion and on 11 June the school was again closed for a further evacuation. As far as the parents were concerned, this order does not seem to have been taken very seriously as only 16 children were registered and by 24 June the school had reopened. It then continued to work under all difficulties, even during the daylight raids.

The log-book records the times of each alert and of the all-clear signals during the school day, and it is quite obvious that the work was seriously affected for several months. Alerts could sound several times a day, 7th and 8th October being particularly trying with no less than four alerts on both occasions. Hours at a time were spent in the shelters, for example, on 16 September from 2.12 to 6pm, on 3 October from 2.20 to 5.20pm and 4 October from 1.20 to 5.40pm. Other warnings were of shorter duration, from 20 to 30 minutes, but it is clear that the classwork was much disrupted and it must also be borne in mind that night raids also affected the childrens' sleep. Staff and pupils both lived in constant tension when survival was really all that mattered.

All these events were over 50 years ago and the children studying the subject have the classroom walls hung with wartime posters, 'Dig for Victory' and 'Idle Talk Costs Lives'. They have carefully weighed out a week's ration of sugar, tea, fat and a solitary egg with a ration book beside it. All new to the young of today, but full of nostalgia to those of us who lived through those years.

Printed September 1992/Newsletter number 122

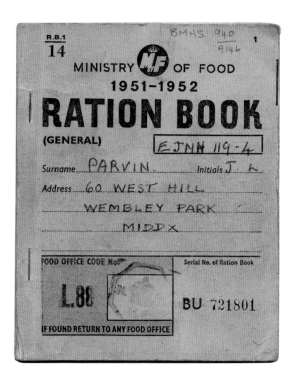

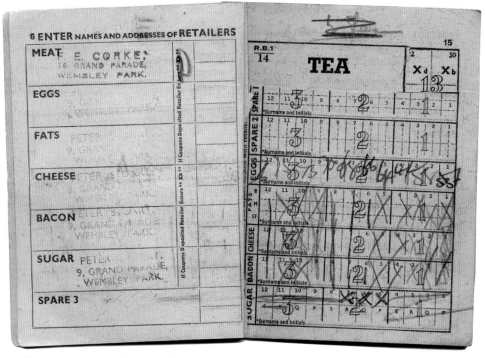

Typical ration books donated to the society

Peace time emergencies

Fire...Fire!

Sometime in 1835 a disastrous fire occurred at the Red Lion, then an old thatched hostelry.

Following this the landlord, Mr William Padgett, gave notice at a Vestry[1] Meeting on November 3rd of that year that at a future meeting he "will move that an Engine be provided for the purpose of extinguishing fires that may accidently (sic) occur in this Parish."

No further mention is recorded on the subject of a fire engine for over thirty years. At length on April 23rd 1867 the matter was again raised "but as no rate could at present be made available for the purpose the matter was withdrawn." This time, however, there must have been a body of agitators as after Christmas the following year the agenda included, among other business, "to consider the propriety of providing a Fire Engine, Ladder and Fire Escape for general use in the Parish." Under the provision of an 1865 Act of Parliament a Metropolitan Fire Brigade was established and probably Barnes residents wished to follow suit. Still the Vestry hedged. Lack of money and a suitable site were offered as excuses but, after correspondence with the Dean and Chapter of St. Paul's[2], and a visit from their land surveyor, it was recommended that the Engine House should be built on the triangular piece of ground opposite the Sun Inn "at which the three roads meet and on which the direction post

Original proposed site for the Engine House

stands." Next, estimates were to be obtained for an engine "similar to one lately purchased by Mortlake Parish." At this stage a local desire not to be outdone by the neighbouring village clearly comes into play until the outlay caused dismay. The estimate ran as follows:

Engine	£112.0.0
Lamps	£ 3.0.0
Cistern	£ 2.2.0
Hose	£ 3.0.0
Sub total	£150.0.0
Fire Escape	£ 22.0.0
Engine House	£300.0.0
Railings	£100.0.0
Total[3]	**£572.0.0**

In addition it would be necessary to appoint a person living in the Parish to be in charge and a volunteer Brigade of enterprising young men would be needed to man the Engine. Bearing the expenses in mind not even local pride was sufficient to encourage the members of the Vestry to continue with the project. They claimed that the cost was too high and the position of the Engine House did not meet with general approval so they wished to drop the business. Clearly there was discord among the inhabitants when they heard that notice had been given to rescind the whole proposition. Some residents must have worked overtime in their anxiety to settle this important matter to their satisfaction and the safety of the community, but only one name is recorded. On April 23rd 1868 it was announced that Mrs Ratcliff (of Rose House[4]) had "donated a Fire Escape to the Parish as a mark of gratitude for not siting the Engine House at the Sun Inn." Undoubtedly a

Parish fire engine and stocks outside The Limes, Mortlake High Street, c.1910

building on the triangle would have been detrimental to her outlook over the pond and green. The Fire Engine was now to be housed on the other side of the pond between the village school on the Green[5] and Elm Cottage. Some years later it was stored in the area now covered by the Dunmow Hall in Station Road. The last reference to this episode is recorded in March 1870 when it was resolved "that the Escape be placed in charge of the Beadle, that he be required to exercise it once a month and keep it in working order. Allowed three guineas p.a. for the duty."

Finally when Barnes and Mortlake merged as an Urban District Council another move was made and a more central situation was designated for the whole area. This was beside The Limes[6] in Mortlake High Street after it had been taken over as the Council House in 1895.

Printed March 1988/Newsletter number 104

[1] Vestry – the local authority of the day.
[2] The Dean and Chapter of St. Paul's – at the time they owned the freehold of Barnes, and had done since the late 10th Century. They were Lords of the Manor of Barnes.
[3] The sums of money are, of course in Pounds, shillings and pence (£.s.d).
[4] Rose House – later to become Barnes Community Association.
[5] School on the Green – now Barnes Social Centre.
[6] The Limes, 123 Mortlake High St, one of the few big houses by the river in Mortlake still remaining today.

The great fire at Barn Elms Farm

The evening of 24 August 1889 was a momentous one for Barnes inhabitants.

Around 9.00pm a labourer noticed a fire on Barn Elms estate which he at first took to be the Manor House itself. Closer observation showed it was on Trowell's[1] Farm which occupied a site on the land at present covered by the west end of the Wild Life sanctuary[2].

In great haste he ran off to Barnes Police Station, about a mile distant, to raise the alarm. The farm premises consisted of a dwelling house and various outbuildings including a large timber built barn which contained the newly reaped wheat and oats. Adjoining was a valuable haystack surrounded by coops of hens and ducks. Barnes Police aroused themselves to action by sending off a telegram to Richmond fire station and messengers to alert the Barnes and Mortlake brigades. As might be expected, Barnes answered promptly and were the first to arrive with their manual appliance, shortly followed likewise by Mortlake.

Meanwhile the flames had taken a strong hold of the barn and it was a considerable relief when Captain Covell from Richmond arrived with his No.2 steamer and took charge. He was soon followed by brigades from Kew, Ham and Chiswick so great was the emergency. At first the water supply proved difficult. The Thames was too far away for the hoses to reach, but fortunately there was sufficient in the lake[3] only 200-300 yards away. This supply enabled the house and other outbuildings to be saved but it was impossible to quench the flames on the barn. While the inmates were removing furniture and belongings from the house, the firemen set to and partially demolished the shed between the house and the haystack.

Meanwhile the news spread quickly and crowds interfered with the firemen's work. Inspector Aldredge rode over from Richmond and ably helped by Sergeant Jones and P.C. Howe of Barnes, they kept order among the dense numbers of onlookers and rendered aid to the brigades. Then, unfortunately, the haystack caught alight and with damage both from fire and water was practically destroyed. The barn, despite the volume of water poured on it, was totally wrecked and only the small foundation remained standing.

By midnight the fire was considered to be under control though the Barnes and Mortlake manuals continued to play upon the smouldering mass for some hours afterwards. The night sky was illuminated for a considerable distance around and caused great excitement outside the immediate vicinity. It was supposed this conflagration was caused by a spark from a labourer's pipe earlier in the evening. The damage which was estimated at £1,000 was covered by insurance in the County Fire Insurance Office. It is difficult to assess the present day value, but presumably it would be anything from £10,000 to £20,000.

Printed February 1990/Newsletter number 112

Barnes Fire Brigade, 1913

[1] Barn Elms Farm – Francis Trowell was the tenant.
[2] London Wetlands Centre.
[3] Part of the lake is still on Barn Elms and is used by the angling club.

Source material
Richmond and Twickenham Times, August 1899, Local Collection.
Richmond Reference Library.

A Christmas Hero

The date of December 24th 1895 must have been remembered by many in Barnes for the remainder of their lives – as they recalled this story of conspicuous and yet practically unrecorded bravery.

On Christmas Eve in the hall attached, at that date, to St. Michael's Church[1], the children who formed the local branch of the Band of Hope held their weekly meeting. A special Christmas entertainment had been devised and one, Florence Weeks, "dressed in a long scarlet robe trimmed with cotton wool and long flowing beard represented Father Christmas." Our hero, the Rev. Percy Wonnacott, warned her carefully beforehand not to go too close to the foot-lights and the whole show was an outstanding success. Herein, indeed, lay the seeds of disaster for the vociferous young audience demanding an encore, Florence excitedly acknowledged the applause and came too near the front of the stage. Suddenly the train of her robe caught the flame of a gas jet with the result that in an instant the poor girl was alight.

Onto the stage rushed our hero and vainly tried to pull Florence onto the floor as, in her terror, she ran round the stage. At length she was controlled and Mr Wonnacott beat out the flames with his bare hands, while members of the audience prevented panic spreading among the young fear-stricken audience. It was only after Florence had been conveyed home and instant medical attention given her for shock and facial burns that her rescuer's serious injuries were realised. Mr Wonnocott's hands were in a shocking state "the right in one place being burnt to the bone". He was taken to the home of Dr Armstrong of 8 Northumberland Avenue[2], and there stayed for nearly a fortnight with the Doctor himself attending to him night and day in his terrible sufferings.

By the end of January he was sufficiently recovered to send a Thank You message "to all those parishioners and friends who so kindly called or sent letters and cards of sympathy and for the many kind gifts of flowers and good things which he thoroughly enjoyed." He went on to thank Dr Armstrong attributing his early recovery to his great skill and devotion and then added humbly that he himself was 'deeply gratified and touched to find that his effort to perform what was, after all, only his duty, should have been so generously recognised.'

At the end of this account it should be recorded that the footlights at the time of the show were in the same condition as when seen by the District Surveyor and passed prior to the granting of the annual licence. However, important alterations were made immediately afterwards which it was considered would render any similar accident well nigh impossible. Of Florence Weeks and Percy Wonnacott there are no further details but Father Christmas can hardly have appeared to them again as the jolly bearer of Christmas Cheer which it is hoped he symbolises to our readers.

Printed December 1976/Newsletter number 59

Florence excitedly acknowledged the applause and came too near the front of the stage. Suddenly the train of her robe caught the flame of a gas jet with the result that in an instant the poor girl was alight.

[1] St Michael and All Angels' Church, Elm Bank Gardens.
[2] This road, in Barnes parish, is close to Gypsy Lane, adjoining the former Northumberland Arms Hotel.

Source
The Parish Gazette for St. Mary's Barnes, Vol. I No. 2. Charles Hailstone Collection.

The Great Barnes Flood

June 1903 proved to be a most unusual month for local residents and one that must have been talked about for many years afterwards.

On Saturday 13th, a steady downpour of rain began, and so heavy was it that by Sunday morning the Pond was brimming over and by Monday 15th, the children who attended the Green School had to make a detour around Church Road to reach their classrooms. The rain continued ceaselessly and later that day the overflowing brook had submerged a portion of the Ranelagh Club grounds at Barn Elms, the Green, Station Road and Beverley Path. The water was level with the Common footbridge and residents in Water Rat Cottage in Station Road had to leave their home.

By Tuesday there had been 60 hours of incessant rain and matters worsened. The Green School was unusable as it was surrounded by 17 inches of water. The caretaker, assisted by a local builder, lifted out cupboards and the stock was preserved, but to do this they waded through several inches of water in the classrooms. Houses were now flooded in Church Road, Ranelagh Avenue and the Crescent, while a punt was requisitioned and a ferry established across the Green between

Cleveland House and Beverley School, now Beverley Close. Houses in Rectory Road, Bellevue Road and portions of Cardigan and Glebe Roads were suffering from the high level of water in the Brook and some residents, wishing to reach the station, took off their shoes and waded along flooded roads carrying a towel in a suitable receptacle. They then stopped on dry ground, wiped their feet and donned their footwear, doubtless reversing the process when coming home.

During this spell no letters were delivered in the flooded areas, but Barnes was not the only district to suffer. Both Mortlake and East Sheen, near the Brook, were similarly affected. Houses in White Hart Lane, Fitzgerald Avenue, Eleanor Grove and the Upper Richmond Road at Priests Bridge were in trouble and Palewell Fields were under water, much to the delight of local children who caught eels in the vicinity. Further afield, Petersham Meadows were submerged and at Richmond Station the water was level with the platform, but it was Beverley Brook

Barnes, Floods, 1903.

Photo by W. Field

Station Road, Barnes, looking towards Church Road

Rustic Bridge, Ranelagh Avenue, Barnes

E. A. Medus and Co., Barnes

The bridge across the Rythe, leading from the Common to Ranelagh Avenue

which caused the greatest local trouble. In all 192 houses were affected and Church Road from Rose Cottage[2] to the Rectory gates (Strawberry House) was under 2 feet of water.

By Friday 19th, an additional pond had formed on the Green, but the worst was passed. Water in the gardens of houses in Beverley Road was receding and the rustic bridge, which crossed the Rythe[3] facing Elm Grove Road, and which had been several feet under water, could now be identified. The great Barnes flood was over.

The outcome of this unusual event bore unexpected fruit. It led to a group of local residents meeting and forming a deputation to approach the Urban District Council on the subject. As they were not considered to be an official collective body they were refused a hearing but, nothing daunted, these enterprising folk formed themselves into the Barnes Ratepayers and Residents Association[4] and as such the Highways Committee took notice of the circumstances, which required considerable attention. This Association continued to play an important part in the social welfare of the locality for very many subsequent decades.

Printed September 1994/Newsletter number 130

---

[1] Water Rat Cottage stood at the end of the present Willow Avenue – see also page 57.
[2] This cottage stood on The Green, opposite Nos 29-35 Church Road. It was later demolished for road widening.
[3] The Rythe – a stream which ran alongside the Beverley Brook, from Barnes to Putney Lower Common. It was filled in during the 1920's.
[4] They became absorbed by the Barnes Community Association in 1980.

Sources

Richmond and Barnes Times, 20 June 1903.
Barnes Urban District Council, Highways Committee minutes 6 July and 5 October 1903.
Handbook of the Barnes and Mortlake Ratepayers Association, 75th Anniversary, 1978.

Barnes Terrace

The Papendiek Family in Barnes

It is only recently that fuller details of Mr and Mrs Christopher Papendiek's connections with Barnes have been brought to light. They were both closely involved with the court life of King George III and Queen Charlotte and moved frequently from residences in Kew, London and Windsor to be in attendance on their Majesties and the ever increasing number of royal children.

Mrs Papendiek kept a voluminous journal which was edited years later by her granddaughter under the title "Court and Private life in the time of Queen Charlotte". Her husband, Christopher, in his capacity as a musician, was almost daily in attendance and after his early death she served her Majesty as assistant Keeper of the Wardrobe and Reader. Thus she was able to write of the daily doings of both her own family and Court occasions.

The first recorded event in this area is of an unfortunate meeting with highwaymen. The Papendieks were returning, with friends, from an "agreeable evening's entertainment" to their home in Kew via Clapham and Barnes being driven in a coach hired from Shrubsole, a livery man at Richmond. "Turning from Barnes Terrace to the beginning of Mortlake Lane[1]" three men ran up from the waterside and while one went to the horses' heads the other two placed themselves on each side of the carriage and opened the doors. Mr Papendiek gave them his purse, which luckily contained little money, but he was forced to alight and be searched. Nothing was found on him but a clasp knife which the miscreant opened and then could not close so he returned it with an oath and the words "Clear the gentleman, we will not disturb the ladies". So saying the coach was allowed to proceed.

The Papendieks made a number of friends in this neighbourhood and especially with the artist Zoffany and his family at Strand-on-the-Green. Mrs Papendiek sat for her portrait but

Mrs Papendiek

did not enjoy being in "a cramped attitude for many hours." Another friendship was that of James and Rebecca Duberly, who resided for a while at East Sheen as well as having a town house. The story of Rebecca's elopement with General Gunning has been fully related in the Society's publication *Barnes and Mortlake People* and was researched by the late Mrs. Jean Wadley, but the Papendieks remained on most friendly terms with James Duberly after his wife had deserted him.

By 1807 the Papendieks were renting No. 7 Barnes Terrace from the owner William Payne. Being members of the Court Staff certainly had its domestic advantages for in the Lord Chamberlain's Ledger, dated February 5th 1808, is the item; – "Men's time at Barnes taking up Drawing Room carpet and from thence in a boat to Hammersmith with carpets taking the plan of Back Drawing Room for carpet etc. and altering ditto, Thread and Incidents used." "Paid them Coach hire and Expenses £1.1.10."

At the same date Charlotte Augusta Papendiek, the eldest child, was living in Milbourne House. She had married, in 1802, Thomas Oom, a wealthy Russian merchant and having had a son born in March 1807 it might have been an inducement for her parents to take the Terrace house so as to be near their daughter and baby grand-son. Thomas Oom died a few years afterwards and Charlotte remarried the Right Honorable Joseph Planta. They returned to Milbourne House in 1818. (See page 10, *Milbourne House, Barnes*, published by the History Society available in the Library.) Joseph's aunt

Margaret Planta, was also employed by her Majesty and there are many references to her in Mrs. Papendiek's journal. This may well account for the acquaintance of her nephew with Charlotte Papendiek.

Christopher Papendiek died some time before his wife but she appears to have been a busy widow and loving mother to her six children. She kept up a close relationship with Queen Charlotte but unfortunately for us died before she had completed her fascinating memoirs.

Printed September 1989/Newsletter number 110

[1] Mortlake High Street was referred to as Lane or just Street in early documents.

Sources

Barnes Land Tax Returns.
Surrey Record office.
Barnes Rate Books.
Local Collection, Richmond Reference Library
Lord Chamberlain's Public Record Office Ledger, Court and Private life in the time of Queen Charlotte: being the journals of Mrs. Papendiek, assistant keeper of the Wardrobe and Reader to her Majesty. Edited by her granddaughter Mrs. Vernon Delves Broughton.
In 2 volumes 1887.

Barnes Terrace c.1800, from a watercolour by J Rowlandson. This scene is where the High Street joins the Terrace, looking west, with Mortlake and Castelnau House in the background

Nurserymen and artists

At the turn of the 19th century, living at Albion House (later Elm Bank) on Barnes Terrace were George Cooke, a line engraver, and his artist son Edward. The Cookes were employed by a famous nurseryman of Hackney, by name George Loddiges, to illustrate a book on horticulture for the firm.

Edward Cooke was much involved in this production and paid a number of visits to Hackney to make the drawings. Business was obviously combined with romance, for Edward married Jane, George Loddiges's daughter, and they took up residence in the Cooke household on Barnes Terrace.

Sadly, the marriage was of fairly short duration for after the fire at St Mary's Church in 1978 a brass plate came to light which had been hidden for many years behind the reredos of the high altar. The inscription runs:

Albion House

> To the glory of God and in memory of
> Jane Cooke, a former resident of this Parish,wife of
> E. M. Cooke R.A. A.R.S. and daughter of George Loddiges
> of Hackney, who died 28th December 1843, aged 31 years.
> This light is dedicated by her nephew George Loddiges of Castelnau.

The centre light of the east window depicting our Lord's resurrection under which it had been placed, was lost in the fire.

Members of the Loddiges family settled in Barnes and gave continuous service to the church and locality. Many of our residents will remember Marjorie Loddiges who, shortly before her death, had given a quantity of daffodil bulbs to be planted under the churchyard wall. Here they are naturalising and are a touching memorial to the two families of nurserymen and artists who, through marriage, had made their home in Barnes.

The brass can now bw seen on the east wall of the rebuilt church.

Printed December 1992/Newsletter number 123

Riverside Delights

Three months after the death at Croydon of Margaret, the nine year old daughter of the poet W.E. Henley, he came with Anna his wife to live at 9 Barnes Terrace.

Expectation rose high for, in a letter dated 30th April 1894, Henley wrote, "the house is going to be a success, at least so far as looks are concerned", and early in May the Henleys moved out to Barnes. By 8th May they were settled and he wrote, "Barnes is lively since we came. A man was murdered on the Common some days back and this morning two bodies were taken out of the river one under my eyes – as it were at our front door".

This house has been altered since the Henleys lived in it. Then it was long and low and the latticed balcony, which overlooked the river, was covered with climbing foliage. Henley was crippled – one reason for a frequent change of house – and from the desk in his first floor study he overlooked the river and the Chiswick meadows beyond. Opposite his study was the drawing room where his many visitors were entertained. One of the first to come was a young writer H.G. Wells, and on Boat Race day there was a gathering of celebrities including Mrs Meynell[1], to whom he had written soon after their arrival, "this is the pleasantest old house and the river is a perpetual miracle", while to William Archer, critic and journalist, he was equally enthusiastic. "Do you know Barnes? If you don't you ought to. We live in a verandah on the river". But the winter brought fog and dampness and their delight waned. The attractiveness of the house was proving deceptive and by the next year Anna began to think of moving on yet again. Henley had "a horrible eczema" which he became convinced was due "to Barnes". On October 15th l895 he wrote, "I am better but in no great shakes. Barnes is really and truly the Devil". It was then too late in the year for Anna to go house hunting so they decided to make the best of a second winter where they were and "take our chance of the spring lettings". Fate was kind and early in 1896, after about two years on Barnes Terrace, the Henleys moved to higher ground on Muswell Hill.

Printed May 1975/Newsletter number 53

[1] Alice Meynell, poet, essayist, and journalist. Sister of Lady Elizabeth Butler, painter of Military subjects. Born Thompson, both lived in Castelnau during childhood, baptised St Mary's, Barnes.

Bibliography

W.E. Henley by L. Cope Cornford. Constable & Co.1915.
W.E. Henley A Memoir by Kennedy Williamson. Harold Shayler 1950.
W.E. Henley by John Connell. Constable & Co. 1949.

Alice Meynell

Henley was reputedly the model for Long John Silver in *Treasure Island* and Margaret his daughter for Wendy in *Peter Pan*. Henley was a friend of both R.L. Stevenson and J.M Barrie.

W.E Henley

Another boat race of long ago

On a more modest scale but just as enjoyable for the spectators seems to have been *an Exciting Scullers' Race for £30* which took place over part of the Championship Course 20 years after the University Boat Race tradition had been established.

Details of the event are recounted in the 1983 Autumn edition of the Journal of the North Middlesex and City of London Family History Society. The contestants, named T. Sutliff and J. Smith, were backed for £30 by their respective firms and the race from Putney to Barnes was held on 23rd September 1865. A craft named Venus was chartered so that friends would have a day of "fun and jollity" and both scullers had considerable expert training beforehand. Sutliff won the toss for choice of station and the betting was 5 to 4 on him. Sutliff quickly obtained the lead. At the London Rowing Club Boat House he was at least two lengths ahead, at Hammersmith about four. Then excitement began in earnest for when the "bathing place at Barnes" was reached Smith was over his opponent's stern. Sutliff made a supreme final effort and finished two lengths in advance. The account finishes by stating the time was 21 minutes 30 seconds which

Lithograph dated October 1859 of Robert Chambers, Champion of England, at Mortlake. On the left is the White Hart, and in the centre above the sculler – The Limes

"was not bad considering the tide was unfavourable".

But in what paper or magazine would this account have originally appeared? If anyone can answer this query kindly let Mary Grimwade know. She will pass on the information to a descendant of Thomas Sutliff who owns the cup presented to him.

Printed May 1984/Newsletter number 89

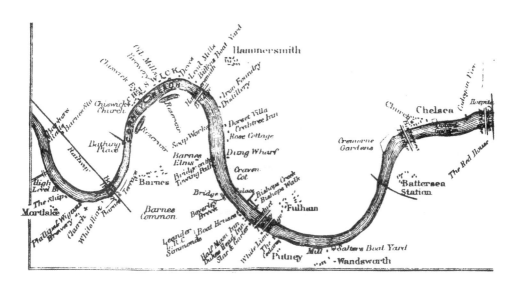

Section of map reproduced in *The Oxford & Cambridge Boat Races 1829 to 1869* by W.F. Macmichael BA, published by Deighton, Bell & Co in 1870, from which information about the early University boat races was obtained (Courtesy Richmond Ref. Library)

Match between Eton and Westminister, 1843. This depicts the conclusion of the race and includes an unusually accurate view of the buildings then existing along the river at Mortlake

Notice the Brewery chimney in the distance

Lesser Barnes authors

Little-known Barnes writers

Many senior citizens may recall the thrills of the film *Beau Geste* shown in pre-World War II days.

The author of the novel from which this was adapted was Major Percival Christopher Wren, JP, MA (Oxon), who lived in Church Road, Barnes for three years after coming down from Oxford. He was then teaching at the Chelsea Pupil Teacher Centre and was described by one of his pupils, who resided locally, as being "always very jolly" and a keen tennis player. Presumably after war service he devoted his time to writing and became a prolific author of adventure books. Probably his best known were *Beau Geste* (1924), *Beau Sabreur* (1926) and *Beau Ideal* (1928). He died at his London address, Albermarle Street, W1, in November 1941.

Another local resident with literary leanings was Miss Clementia Black of Westmoreland Road who died in December 1922.

She was the daughter of a town clerk of Brighton and earned fame not only as a writer, but as a "tireless worker in the cause of poorer members of her sex." A member of the Executive Committee of the London Society for Women's Suffrage, she was granted a Civil List pension "in recognition of services to the amelioration of the conditions of industrial employment of women." Among her writings were a novel entitled *Caroline* (John Murray, 1908), and a biography, *The Linleys of Bath* (Martin Seeker, 1911). This latter work was written in Hampstead according to the foreword.

Printed September 1994/Newsletter number 130

Joseph Comyns Carr (1849-1916)

In the book *Some Eminent Victorians* the author, Joseph Comyns Carr, refers to his childhood in the Manor House on Barnes Common. This had formerly been the Barnes Workhouse until 1836 and the site is now occupied by the block of flats on the triangle of land bounded by Queens Ride and the Upper Richmond Road.

The Workhouse on Barnes Common, later a private residence known as The Manor House

Joseph's career was subsequently of considerable interest in the world of the theatre, art and literature. He wrote some not very successful plays, but his reputation was built up by his connection with important magazines of his day. He contributed to the *Pall Mall Gazette*, the *Art Critic*, and was the founder and the editor of the *English Illustrated Magazine*. In *Some Eminent Victorians* there are references to a number of people in this area with whom he had contact. These include his school friend William Terriss[1], the German Reeds[2], Julia Cameron[3], with whom he stayed in the Isle of Wight, and Walter Crane[4]. Yet more important still was the encouragement he gave to a young book illustrator, Hugh Thomson, himself a resident in the Richmond locality. At Carr's suggestion, Thomson drew delightful vignettes for the 1896 production of *Days with Sir Roger de Coverley*. In this he used such scenes as the interior of Petersham Church with its box pews, Ham House and the exterior of St Mary's, Barnes. In 1908 he joined with Eric Parker to illustrate *Highways and Byways in Surrey*, long out of print but well worth looking for as a collector's item.

Printed May 1975/Newsletter number 53

As a child, Carr records that the gardens and adjoining fields were an earthly paradise to a family of ten children while the Common, covered with gorse and bracken, was an even wider playground. Each October the children gathered material for a bonfire on 5 November, keeping a watchful eye lest authority should come down on them for removing Common undergrowth. Collecting this material brought them into conflict with the village boys whom they entitled "the cads" and with whom they waged ceaseless warfare. If possible, "the cads" would light the pile of brushwood before the appointed night and thus ruin the celebrations. Carr also has memories of an elder cousin in scarlet uniform walking along the footpath to Barnes station en route to war in the Crimea. In the Vestry minutes for 1862 it is recorded that Carr's father gave notice that he would only be remaining in the house until the end of the year. Mr Carr is stated by John Eustace Anderson to have been a city woollen merchant and his son implies that with a family of ten children there was little money to spare, although he seems to have had a happy childhood.

[1] William Terriss – Actor and Barnes resident. Assassinated outside the Adelphi Theatre 1897.
[2] German Reed – East Sheen resident. Entertainer.
[3] Julia Cameron – East Sheen resident. Photographer.
[4] Walter Crane – Artist and book illustrator.

A prolific writer

At the turn of the century there lived in Scarth Lodge, 1 Scarth Road, Barnes, an extremely prolific writer of light fiction, John Bloundelle-Burton.

By 1903 he had no less than 17 titles listed at the beginning of yet another novel, *A Branded Name*. Many of his stories had a sea-going background, bearing such titles as *Across the Salt Seas, The Desert Ship, The Seafarers* and *The Silent Shore*. Indeed the one entitled *The Hispaniola Plate*, written in 1899, was reviewed by *The Scotsman* as "A tale of piracy and treasure seeking, heaped up, pressed down and running over with buccaneers, sharks and foul weather", while the *Literary World* declared, "It can be recommended to young and old alike for a vigorous and well-constructed story of exciting adventure in lawless times, rounded off with a charming and no less stirring modern romance."

Another of his works of fiction first appeared as a serial in *The Family Circle*, but was later published in book form. *The Pall Mall Gazette*, reviewing *The Day of Adversity*, described it as an historical romance in the days of Louis XIV and went on to say, "The first part of the book is almost as good as if written by Stanley Weyman... The description of the attack upon the slave galley is very good." This fascination with nautical matters seems strange in a man who was educated for the Army and had spent some years of his life in Canada and a variety of European countries. In the *Richmond Herald* of 5 October 1894 an article appeared about the writer which stated that Mr John Bloundelle-Burton lived in a comfortable, roomy house called Scarth Lodge on Barnes Common, the principal charm of which was: "That I can walk out on the grass of the Common from my garden, that I have no opposite neighbours and that a fast train will take me to town or bring me back in 20 minutes. Also because various members of my family have dwelt in the neighbourhood for many years."

In addition to writing novels, Bloundelle-Burton was a journalist and reporter. A letter has come to hand written on 3 August 1895 when he was travelling on *HMS Empress of India*, Channel Squadron. This was to a literary agent Grant Reid and he states that he was acting as Special Correspondent for the *Standard* newspaper during manoeuvres. His earlier works were published by Cassell & Company Limited and his later by Methuen & Company. They are rarely heard of, seen or read today, but there is a collection in the London Library from which they are infrequently borrowed. In his entry in *Who Was Who*, no less than 32 of his works are named. John Bloundelle-Burton died at 385 Upper Richmond Road, Putney, in 1917.

Printed March 1999/Newsletter number 148

Horse dealing in Barnes

Sir Francis Hastings Doyle 1810-88 Professor of poetry at Oxford University, lived for a short span of years at Cleveland House, Barnes Green. The following extract from his autobiography, although undated by him, would probably have occurred some time in the 1860's.

"I owned a big, powerful animal, sixteen hands high, but unfortunately broken-winded, and with forelegs open to criticism. As I had let my house for a year I wanted to get rid of him; he was sold, after a good deal of chaffering, to the cabman at Barnes Station for four pounds. Unluckily I did not insist upon having the money paid down there and then; the consequence was, that during a visit to James Wortley[1] at Mortlake, the butler interrupted me in the middle of my soup by announcing that a man in the hall wished to speak to me on particular business. When I went out I found my friend the cabman, who kept repeating that the horse had bitterly disappointed him. In vain I suggested that you could not expect to buy a Derby winner for four pounds. Admitting that, he still was determined not to fulfill his engagement, and as I had no place, except my bedroom, to lodge the horse in, I had to accept his terms and let the beast go for thirty shillings, the market value of his hide."

Printed September 1973/Newsletter number 46

[1] Sir James Stuart-Wortley lived in East Sheen Lodge. 1856-7 Solictor General under Lord Palmerston.

Cleveland House Academy, later a private house, demolished in 1926. Site now occupied by The Old Sorting Office (O.S.O.)

Local Eccentrics

An Eccentric Barnes Farmer

William Cobbett, 1766-1855 was Surrey born and bred.
He was proud of his humble parentage and first appeared in this
neighbourhood when he walked a great part of the way from
Farnham to see for himself the attractions of Kew Gardens. That
was to prove one of the least of his life-long excursions which
involved travelling in America and riding all over England.

After a gap of years he reappeared in this area when, in October 1827, he began farming at Barn Elms. His land is now covered by The Wetlands Centre. Here he conducted a variety of experiments both in farming method and mode of living. When he took over the land was in poor condition and needed thorough turning and digging. In order to help unemployment, prevalent at that time, he determined to rely solely on human labour, and, with this end in view, inserted an advertisement in his paper *The Political Register* of December 15th 1827 inviting any man who wanted a spell of hard honest toil to come to his farm. No ploughs would be used there and work was to begin at daylight and end at sunset (although this was later amended so as to fix a specific quota). The men would be taken on and paid daily in kind consisting of two pounds of bread, half a pound of cheese and two pounds of meat. This was worth considerably more than normal wages could buy so they could sell the surplus to cover lodging and other needs. Artfully this cost Cobbett nothing because the goods were produced on the farm. Apparently he had no difficulty in getting labourers and he argued this was not serfdom as the men were free to leave at any time.

Cobbett's farm at Barn Elms

Another experiment at Barnes was his crop of Indian corn (maize) or "Cobbett's Corn" as it was popularly called. (This is now know as Corn on the Cob.) He had brought back seeds from America but failed in persuading the public to use it as a substitute for potato even though he published a number of *The Register* on paper made from the husks to attract attention to its varied possibilities.

Cobbett loved birds and animals and regretted that at Horncastle, in Lincolnshire, there was a want of singing birds. "At this moment (five o'clock in the morning) the groves at Barn Elm (sic) are echoing with the warblings of thousands and thousands of birds". He goes on to list thrush, blackbird, lark, white-throat or nettle-torn and "all the rest begin the moment the sun gives the signal". Here, too, he kept "a very diminutive mare, on which my children had all in succession learned to ride, and she is now at Barn Elm (sic) about twenty-six years old and I daresay as fat as a mole."

This homestead was run, in Cobbett's frequent absences, by Mr Dean, who appears to have remained a faithful friend even when the Barnes establishment was given up late in 1851. Dean's name appears among the list of mourners at Cobbett's funeral at Farnham nearly four years later. During Cobbett's tenure twelve people lived at the house in Barnes. These included him and his wife, seven children, Mr Dean and two maidservants.

Printed September 1975/Newsletter number 54

Bibliography

The Life of William Cobbett – dedicated to his sons, published by F.J. Mason, 444 West Strand, 1835.
Memoirs of the late William Cobbett Esq. by Robert Huish. Published by John Saunders, 25 Newgate St. 1836, 2 Vols.
The Life and Letters of William Cobbett in England and America by Lewis Melville, Published John Lane. 1912, 2 Vols.

Old Parr

Old Parr, or to give his full name George Augustus Parr, kept a library and stationer's shop in the mid-nineteenth century at Number 1, Church Road, Barnes.

On Sundays he entertained visitors and these included such folk as the novelist Charles Dickens, Benjamin Webster, actor and theatre manager, Paul Bedford, actor and opera singer and Joseph Seeley, a solicitor from the Bedford Row area of London. Seeley may very possibly have been connected with the publishing business of that name in Fleet Street.

Miss Mary Attwell, when a child, frequently went to the shop with her father and was greatly in awe of the weird figure that emerged from the dark interior. He was dressed in a long overcoat or gaberdine, open at the throat and collarless which must have been unusual to her in the l870's. His reddish grey hair was long and scanty and his eyes were red-rimmed so that she felt he was a kind of wizard. This idea was heightened by the atmosphere of the shop which exuded an alarming and uncanny feeling.

Old Parr ordered books and pamphlets for his customers and discussed literary, political and theological questions with Professor Attwell. Bolton Corney, the well known bibliophile, who lived in a house on Barnes Terrace, was another customer as was also Dr. John Doran. This latter gentleman was the editor of two literary magazines and the author of several publications, one of which was an historical account of the English stage entitled *Their Majesties Servants*. Old Parr has long since disappeared from the Barnes scene but his shop still stands, close to the Sun Inn, having served a variety of purposes since his day.

Printed March 1983/Newsletter number 84, Article 1

Old Parr's shop, now a children's outfitters

Old Reuben

Old Reuben died in September 1951 at the advanced age of ninety. He came to Barnes from Suffolk some fifty years previously and set up business as a butcher at 66, Railway Street, now Westfields Avenue.

His full name was Reuben Bell and his East Anglian dialect and charm of manner delighted the residents on his arrival. He soon became a noted figure in the vicinity as he personally delivered the meat to his customers with a butcher's tray on his shoulder and his pet lamb following behind, while in earlier days he had had a pet goose waddling by his side.

He had grown so accustomed to wearing his apron that, even when he was no longer able, through age, to serve the locality with meat he continued to dress each morning in his butcher's gear and, thus arrayed, sat before the fire to read the paper. After his retirement his small active figure, his friendly manner, twinkling eye and merry face was sadly missed by his many friends and customers. He had been in his day a good billiards and bagatelle player and was altogether an unique character in Barnes at the end of the 19th and beginning of the 20th centuries.

Two people have given more information of this unusual butcher. One was Mr. Sedgwick, a former neighbour, and the other Mrs. Dunham, his great-grand-daughter, who lived with the family during her childhood years.

The Bell family consisted of four sons and four daughters, two of the boys following in their father's trade. There was a slaughter house at the rear of the premises and there, heifers, sheep and pigs were killed by Bell so that customers were assured of fresh meat in pre-refrigeration days. Mrs. Dunham recalled helping to make sausages at 5 a.m. with freshly chopped herbs mixed by her great-grandfather, bread, meat and home prepared skins. Both informants spoke of his many pets, Jack, the dog, Mary, the pet lamb, who lived in the kitchen, Peg Woffington, the goose, and the hens which ran freely around the yard and came into the house through the ever open back door. Reuben Bell played billiards and bagatelle at the Hare and

Reuben Bell

Hounds, East Sheen, and, although not an angler himself, helped the local fishermen by supplying them regularly with live bait which he bred in a special tank in the yard.

In addition to news about Reuben Bell, Mr. Sedgwick had further information to give. For many years he worked for the local Council as a rat-catcher, using ferrets and terriers, and in addition eradicated vermin and wasps' nests. During World War II his activities took him all over southern England working for the Ministry of Defence in a large team of operators.

Reuben Bell's Butchers shop, 66 Railway Street.

How little most of us knew of the essential nature of such an occupation in making a vital contribution to the war effort.

Printed March 1983/Newsletter number 84, Article 2

Information for Article 1: *The Barnes and Mortlake Herald,* January 1st, January 22nd, 1927. – *Dictionary of National Biography.*

Information for Article 2: *The Barnes and Mortlake Herald,* September 26th, 1931.

Hermitage Cottage and Monk Lewis

Hidden away from sight but reached from Goodenough Lane, now Grange Road, was Hermitage Cottage. Here from about 1801 until his death seventeen years later lived the poet Matthew Lewis, nicknamed 'Monk' Lewis.

He was an eccentric with an unusual following of friends and acquaintances whom he entertained in his *bijou* retreat and miniature grounds. The Duchess of York drove over from Oatlands, Walter Scott came to dinner and "a numerous party of the young nobility" enjoyed his hospitality at a *déjeuner á la fourchette*. He wrote lengthy letters to his mother during his Barnes years describing his residence, troubles with his servants, his cats, Minnette and Jenny, and the little spaniel Polly which was a present from the Duchess on one of his visits to Oatlands. Lewis died and was buried at sea in May 1818 while returning from a visit to Jamaica where his large fortune was invested in two sugar estates.

Printed in Occasional Paper 9, *Lost Properties in Barnes*

Matthew Gregory Lewis 1775-1818. Author of *The Monk* and *Castle Spectre*. Performed at Drury Lane.

The Arab boy

Henry Scarth, solicitor, owned land in Putney on the north side of the Upper Richmond Road. A great traveller, he returned from a tour of Turkey with a young Arab boy as his servant, by name Yussef Sirree. The public house in the Upper Richmond Road called 'The Arab Boy' was named after him.

Later, Scarth moved to a wooden cottage on Mill Hill, Barnes Common – one time named The Rosary, now Trock's Cottage[1]. He lived there with his servant from 1859 to 1870.

This is an extract from Henry Scarth's will:

"I bequeath to my servant Joseph Sirry whom I brought with me from Btpont (?) in Syria many years since, the sum of £2,000, and also the further sum of £50 to pay his voyage home (whether he goes or not) the same legacies to be paid to him free of legacy duty and declare this to be in full for all wages which I may owe him at the time of my decease, and I hope and trust and enjoin him to be careful of it that it may support and comfort him in his declining years".

From the Census Returns of 1871 it appears that Sirry (sic) stayed on at the cottage as a boarder. An inscription on his grave in Barnes Common Cemetery[2] reads: "In memory of Joseph Sirry late of Mill Hill, native of Syria, who died 5th June, 1880, aged 51 years." His grave is distinct from others in the cemetery in that it is at an angle facing towards Mecca.

Sirree in turn left money and the Rosary to Alice Sims, a teacher at the Green School. In 1888 she married Mr Beard who was still there in 1941. That year he was interviewed by a Herald reporter and his reminiscences were printed in the local press. Probably residents, like me, will remember seeing him sitting, on many occasions, under his rose covered verandah as we passed the cottage.

Printed December 1985/Newsletter number 95

[1] Joseph Cooper, pianist, renamed The Rosary Trock's Mill Cottage after William Trock, the last miller on Mill Hill.
[2] Barnes Common Cemetery is on Rocks Lane.

Philip de Waal

There must be only a few residents in Barnes today who can claim to have known Philip Henry Overbeck de Waal, curate of St. Mary's Church from 1894 to 1923. Not only is his the longest recorded curacy in the history of that church, but surely, too, he must be numbered among the eccentrics of his day.

He came to Barnes as a young deacon and served Canon Kitson continuously until the latter's death. As a child I constantly encountered him for we were close neighbours, he living in the Rectory and I in the road named after his incumbent. He certainly knew my parents but I cannot recall any conversations between him and me. I was probably aware of his unusual appearance and felt shy before him and I doubt whether he felt equal to speaking to little girls. All his life in Barnes he was never seen out of doors without his

All his life in Barnes he was never seen out of doors without his black silk hat, frock coat, white gloves and untidily furled umbrella.

black silk hat, frock coat, white gloves and untidily furled umbrella. He wore steel-rimmed spectacles and his white-haired, erect figure paced the Barnes streets with an absence of hurry peculiar to his generation.

I now suspect he had ritualistic tendencies which the Canon curbed, but every Sunday afternoon, for a number of years, I went regularly to a children's service in which he was free to indulge his private whims. It seems, in retrospect, that he always contrived an excuse for a procession round the church, when, wearing a biretta and suitably robed in an embroidered cope, he clasped his hands, closed his eyes and by the aid of two little boys holding the corners of this vestment was safely steered along the aisle and nave back to the sanctuary. Meanwhile we always sang the same hymn – Ancient & Modern No. 450

Every Friday evening in Lent we were urged to attend an extra service and for this we were rewarded by a small piece of mauve card (correct liturgical colour) containing a single letter, until the sixth week we spelled out the word 'Repent'. If we could hand back the completed word we were given an Easter card to keep. A few years ago, when turning out, I found a few of these letters, probably some childish complaint like chicken-pox had robbed me of complete attainment, but I no longer have any of the final prizes by me.

The Barnes spinsters competed for the opportunity of accompanying him on his daily perambulations and spent a considerable amount of their abundant leisure dodging around Church Road corners hoping to meet him 'unexpectedly'. Gossip reported that there were nearly as many teachers as children in the Sunday School he conducted on Barnes Green, but if there was an iota of truth in that I think he was oblivious of the fact. As a child I thought of him as a lonely person and probably he was, for he apparently spent his spare time studying. Having acquired a London University B.A. degree

two years before his ordination, he became a B.Sc. in 1913. He also wrote detective stories which he had privately printed and one of which, *The Mystery of the Green Garnet Murder*, came into our household many years later.

When the Rev. Patrick Dott succeeded Canon Kitson in 1923, Mr de Waal moved to Acton Green and by 1927 was curate at St. Paul's Oxford, where he stayed until his death in 1941. The last time I saw him was shortly before the outbreak of the second world war. I was sitting in a tea shop close to Paddington Station when he looked in through the window. His black silk hat was now green with age, his fingers were through his white gloves and he still wore a frock coat and clutched an umbrella. I hoped he would come in and I would speak to him at last and tell him I still lived in Barnes. Alas, he turned away – maybe to catch a train to Oxford. I had seen the last of the Victorian clergy, one with forty-seven years faithful service as a humble, under-paid Church of England curate. Nevertheless he was one who, by his individuality had so impressed me that I can recall him clearly on the fiftieth anniversary of his departure from Barnes.

Printed September 1973/Newsletter number 46

Gossip reported that there were nearly as many teachers as children in the Sunday School he conducted on Barnes Green…

Parish and people

1889 – and all that

Through the kindness of a former Barnes resident I have recently been loaned a bound copy of St. Mary's Barnes parish magazine for 1889. Apart from much interesting church news such as the services, list of preachers and the frequent printing of one of the Rector's sermons (Rev. L.T. Lochee), there is much valuable material for the local historian.

In January an item appears giving notice of a soup kitchen in Westfields to be opened during the winter on Tuesdays and Thursdays at 12a.m. (sic). The soup was 1d. a quart and tickets of this price could be bought from Mr Barton[1], High Street, and given to the poor. The following month an announcement stated that the demand on this kitchen had been so great that close upon 250 quarts had proved insufficient and another copper had been added. The Rector asked for contributions towards its cost.

Many organisations helped the less fortunate folk and the Sick Provident Club, Clothing Club, Ladies Association for Befriending Young Children and Blanket Club are some of those continually mentioned. Miss Maples of the Manor House ran a sewing class "for the purpose of providing a safe and useful evening's employment for the poorer and more neglected girls in the parish." One wonders just how many availed themselves of this amenity. Edifying societies also centred round the Church, not least "The Recreative Evening Classes Association." Professor Attwell was the Honorary Treasurer while, strangely enough, his thirty-year old unmarried daughter, Mary, ran the Mother's Meeting.

Barnes High Street, looking west, c.1910
Miss Tallemach (tobacconist), Post and Telegraph Office, Glover (baker), Simpson (printer)

A sad aspect of the magazine is the record of the frequent burials of the many young children. That year practically one third of the total number printed were under five years old, while the majority have entered by their name the age in days or months and not in years at all.

A parish library flourished containing over 1,000 volumes. It was open on Mondays at noon in the Church House and on payment of half-a-crown a year as an Honorary Subscriber, or one penny a month paid in advance, one was able to use it. If a book was damaged a fine of from 1d. to 6d. was levied and no further books could be borrowed until this was paid.

Sunday School Treats seemed to have centred round the Crystal Palace, plans were going ahead for the "proposed new church in Westfields," a fund was afoot for the Hornidge Memorial Window in the chancel,

(Mr Hornidge had been a churchwarden of long standing) and the Vestry were applying for three acres of Common land from the Ecclesiastical Commissioners to extend the Cemetery. This plan failed to materialise.

The magazine generally gives an overall picture of the activities of a caring community. The parish was methodically divided into twenty-four districts and a full list was printed in August 1889 with the streets assigned to each District Visitor. She presumably delivered parish magazines and kept a friendly eye on the less well to do members of the flock. It was all very Victorian, but, in many ways, a more personal approach than that of our present Welfare State.

Printed September 1972/Newsletter number 42

[1] Mr Barton, a long standing churchwarden, owned a draper's shop in the High Street.

A Kindly Act

"It is a matter of common knowledge that the Rector[1] has recently lost his bicycle, which was stolen from the Parish Room by some unknown marauder."

As June 22nd was the Rector's birthday, it occurred to a few friends that it would be a graceful way of recognising the occasion by presenting him with a new machine to replace the abstracted one. The necessary funds were promptly raised within a week, and a beautiful new machine, with all modern improvements, was presented to the Rector as a birthday gift. He was much touched and gratified at this act of thoughtful kindness, and desired that his warmest thanks should be conveyed to all the donors, who naturally wished their gift to be considered as anonymous.

The Rector found the bicycle of great service to him, "not only as a means of taking exercise, but it saves much valuable time when he has to take distant work, e.g. at the Board of Guardians, or to make distant calls."

Printed September 1978/Newsletter number 66

From the July 1896 issue of *St. Mary's, Barnes Parish Gazette.*

[1] The Rector was the Revd B.M.Kitson

The Bad Old Days

1894 would appear to have been a difficult year for the local working population. No unemployment pay, sick benefit, or supplementary allowances and no pensions made life intolerable for those in need.

The Editor of the Richmond Herald printed the following letter explaining that there had been no alteration in the text:-

A Complaint from Barnes Labourers:-

Sir, Hoping you would find room in your valuable paper for this letter on behalf of the workmen of Barnes. In this case which we have cause to complain, is the Barnes man cannot get employment and for why, in the first place the Workmen of Mortlake get it, when it was talked about the Barnes people were going to do the work in Mortlake they grumbled the Mortlake people i mean, I should think that when finished in their own parish they did not ought to come to Barnes to do ours. there are plenty of men in Barnes who want Bread, me for one and if things go on like they are at present we shall have to want. Now in your parish of Richmond i hear that every man haves a chance. And I consider they ought to do the same here. On one or two occasions which i have known if we ask for a job, our foreman will have the Cheek to turn round and say He don't want no giddy young Men and men which I have known to have 5 or 4 children like myself. But we must Remind this gentlemen that we must all live. And the people wonder at crime, would it not make a man do anything when he goes home and then hear his children crying for Bread. There i do not suppose that that counts. I hope that someone will take notice of this and try and do justice to all.
I am yours Respectfully.

A Barnes LABOURER.

In the issue of December 14th 1894 Mr H. Keane of Castelnau replied. He suggested that the local authorities should institute a Labour Register to be kept at the offices of the District Council to enable those requiring work to enter their names, addresses and occupations. One feels that Mr Keane should be remembered as an early instigator of the Labour Exchange.

Printed May 1976/Newsletter number 57

Vivat Regina – 1897

In December 1896 the Rector of Barnes, the Rev. B.M.Kitson, writing in the Parish Gazette asked for suggestions for the most fitting "Parish Sexagenary Memorial" to commemorate Queen Victoria's Diamond Jubilee. Replies came quickly and the following month he reported that a consensus of opinion was in favour of the erection of a Parish Hall.

There was a hall used by St. Michael's people in Archway Street, but that appeared in imminent danger of collapse. The idea was to have a substantial brick building with a basement containing a kitchen (for the cooking of soup, children's dinners and preparing Parish Teas), rooms on the ground floor for classes and committee meetings, and above that a spacious hall for social gatherings and entertainments. This ambitious scheme would also provide an opportunity to enlarge the Parish Library. A plot of ground was vacant at the upper end of Cleveland Road, centrally placed for both churches, and a Committee was formed to look into the project.

By April 1897 the Committee had run into difficulties as the cost of the land was prohibitive, and although the Rector offered an alternative site "on the Glebe land, facing the main road", the Parishioners felt the expense of the building was too high. An alternative plan was agreed on "to complete the Peal of Bells, and to provide a flag-staff and National Banner for the St. Mary's Church Tower." At St. Michael's it was hoped a Choir Vestry and Organ Chamber would be built. In addition merry-making was afoot. Local organisations prepared concerts and entertainments and on June 23rd, the day after the London Festivities, Barnes was to be en fête from morning to night. Actually the day began at 9.45 a.m. with a school procession headed by the Rector in "full University Costume". The children marched from Westfields, by a devious route, to St. Mary's where the 'Royal Ensign' floated from the new flag-staff. Here an ecumenical service of Thanksgiving took place and then on to a great Dinner at "the Mansion of St. Ann's[1]", loaned for the occasion by the London School Board. In a spacious hall in the grounds about 800 "of our poorer and deserving neighbours" sat down to huge joints of beef, legs of mutton, ham, meat pies, salad, bread, beer, and some fifty to sixty plum puddings. A Military band played and proceeded later, with any who wished, to spend the afternoon in the Rectory Fields.

At 4.50 p.m. an estimated 2,000 children sat down in the grounds of St. Ann's to tea, being waited on, as were the diners, by a voluntary band of ladies wearing Union Jack aprons. Maypole dancing, games and swings provided the entertainment and, at a later hour, an Illuminated Bicycle Procession wound through the streets finishing at Priory Lodge[2], where Mr Edward Terry's[3] daughters awarded the prizes for the decorations.

As darkness fell the island on the Pond was lit up with fairy lights, fireworks blazed and twinkled and a bonfire was lit on the Green. Nor was this quite all, for there was sufficient food left from the Feast to distribute the next day to 250 families.

The total expenses of this great celebration amounted to £284.12.0d. the bells costing a further £550. The first peal was rung on them on August 8th 1897 by a band of ringers from Mortlake Parish Church. All these outgoings were met by voluntary contributions and the list of donors and full details of expenditure were printed in the Parish Gazette. Mr J. Williams of Beverley Road, who had acted throughout as the Secretary to the Committee was presented with "a handsome timepiece", which apparently was much appreciated. But there was not sufficient money for any building at St. Michael's and that scheme took another two years before completion and even longer before it was finally paid for.

Printed March 1977/Newsletter number 60

Above: The Williams family in the garden of their house 'The Hollies' on Beverley Road.
Below: The house seen from the front.

The house was bombed and flats now occupy the site

[1] St Ann's house and grounds occupied the area facing the river at Lonsdale Road.

[2] Priory Lodge was a detached house in Church Road facing St. Mary's Church.

[3] Edward O'Connor Terry was an actor and proprietor of Terry's Theatre in the Strand. He lived at Priory Lodge from 1890 till his death in 1912. There is a lovely *Spy* Cartoon of Terry at Orleans House Gallery.

Memories of Essex House

Mrs Ivie, a former Barnes resident, has sent us some interesting and delightful reminiscences of her family connections with Essex House. Her grandparents, Dr and Mrs Henry Hamilton, arrived at the house in 1903 "complete with a family, several horses and a pack of hounds."

Her mother who was then six years old, remembers "how the hounds, found to be surplus to requirements in Barnes were very soon dispatched back to the country while Dr Hamilton, for many years, did his rounds on horseback."

At that time the property was rented at £80 p.a. and comprised Essex House, Old Essex House and the stables, now known as Essex Lodge. In addition there was about an acre of garden stretching from the frontage on Station Road to Stanton Road behind. Old Essex House contained the domestic quarters and showed evidence of Tudor brickwork in the cellar.

When the Hamiltons moved into the house there was a drawing room linked to the dining room by folding doors so that they became a ballroom for festive occasions, and in addition a billiard room. The garden, however, was certainly one of the delights of the residence. It contained both a croquet lawn and a tennis court divided from each other by a great copper beech and a chestnut tree. A very high wall at the end of the grounds was the back of the blacksmith's forge in Stanton Road.

Mrs Hamilton was cousin to John Redmond who became leader of the Irish Party in the House of Commons in 1891 after the fall of Charles Parnell. When the House was sitting he spent weekends from 1903 onwards at Essex House. Like Redmond, Mrs Hamilton was a Roman Catholic and, with her like-minded friend Mrs Moran who lived on Mill Hill, persuaded Bishop Amigo to purchase property in Castelnau where the first Roman Catholic Church in Barnes was established. This has now been rebuilt as St Osmund's. Mrs Ivie's mother, Maud Hamilton, married Dr Hector Smith who assisted his father-in-law in the practice. Mrs Ivie was born in a house in the Crescent but shortly afterwards her parents returned to Essex House until it was sold after Dr Hamilton's death. Later they occupied Old Essex House and then moved away in 1931 selling the property to Dr Brian Lawn. She remembers, as a child, many of the High Street shops and local characters. There was the lamplighter, the muffin man and "old Togni" the iceman. He came down from the iceworks in Hammersmith with his horse and cart laden with great blocks of ice, some of which were delivered weekly to the family at Essex House. In addition his customers included the local fishmongers who laid out their stock-in-trade on marble slabs surrounded with chunks of ice.

Mrs Ivie recalls the Misses Ratcliff who were next door neighbours, not forgetting their Manchester terriers, the plays at Barnes Theatre and polo at Ranelagh Club. There was also a memorable occasion when the river flooded and swept up the High Street to the gate of the house and general indignation when John Barker[1] built the Zeeta Chocolate factory next to the Methodist Church in Station Road[2] and overlooking the Pond and Green.

We are most grateful to Mrs Ivie for recalling these memories and thus adding such interesting background information to Barnes life before World War II.

Printed September 1985/Newsletter number 94

[1] Barker's did not build the Chocolate Factory – Zeeta's The Chocolate and Cake Manufacturers, built it on the site of Cleveland House in 1927. Having demolished the house they sold out to Barker's who only wanted the trade name and closed the factory in 1958.

[2] This site is now occupied by the Old Sorting Office Development (O.S.O.)

Above: Charley Wheatley - the Barnes Lamplighter
Right: Essex House and Old Essex House,
as they are today

Barnes and Mortlake en Fête

Local government of yesterday found time and money for celebrations, in a fashion cash-starved local authorities of today might find hard to believe. Such a day came on September 14, 1932, when the district of Barnes and Mortlake received a Royal charter, and became The Borough of Barnes.

During the week, many special events took place, including a regatta, with an entry of more than 70 competitors; an Empire Shopping Week offering prizes for window-dressing; and an historical pageant and procession through the main streets. Schoolchildren celebrated with sports and tea at a variety of venues, while those attending infant departments were given flags to wave at the procession.

Three hundred "old folk resident within the borough" were entertained at a meat tea (that evocative phrase of plenty!) in the grounds of the Council House[1]. Street decorations and floodlighting added to the scene, while the proprietor of the Ranelagh Cinema[2] in Church Road, Barnes, screened Empire films at a special children's showing.

Another highlight was set up in the Barnes Station goodsyard. The Lord Collingwood, the latest express passenger locomotive, was on display, complete with third-class corridor coaches, all to be visited for one penny. This was exceptionally popular: on Charter Day, more than 3,000 paid for admission, with nearly 8,000 altogether visiting the exhibit. Children in an age when "Steam was King" delighted in exploring the foot-plate and seeing how the giant worked. Proceeds went to charity.

Fireworks rightly completed Charter Day, set off from the Chiswick bank so that citizens of the new borough could have a clear view, the display enhanced by reflections rippling on the Thames.

Even by the Depression values of 1932 – when labour costs would have been modest – the celebrations must have been a major item on the expenditure accounts for the new Borough Councillors to approve. Today it is quite impossible to imagine any such

festivities being offered to the people of the Greater London Borough of Richmond Upon Thames, as they monitor continuing cutbacks in social services and general amenities, with civic pride no longer a matter of concern.

Local government in Barnes, Mortlake and East Sheen has progressed from the concern of the Vestry, to the Urban District Council, then to a Borough, and lastly a Greater London Borough. Inevitably this has cost so much of the sense of community and *esprit de corps* which was joyously expressed by the people of Barnes and Mortlake, even in those grim economic times of 1932.

Printed March 2001/Newsletter number 156

[1] The Council House was The Limes in Mortlake High Street, which still stands, leased as office premises.

[2] Now Olympic Studios.

Information obtained from:

Barnes & Mortlake Herald September 3-10-17-24, 1932.
Evening Standard, Evening News and
The Star September 14 1932.
Daily Telegraph September 12-15 1932.
Daily Mail September 12-15 1932.
The Times September 15 1932.

William Turner's painting of The Limes

Parish and people

Ranelagh Cinema

Contempory Cinema poster from the 1930's

45

Not For Ourselves Alone

In July 1937 the Abbey Publicity Service published an official Guide to Barnes, Mortlake and East Sheen. This booklet, price sixpence, contained 52 pages (12 of which were illustrations), a most comprehensive map with a street index and a coloured cover showing the Borough coat of arms in glorious technicolour with the motto below in quarter inch lettering.

The information given makes fascinating reading today. I am not referring to historical items on the Mortlake Tapestry Works, Potteries or Milbourne House, but rather to the incidental facts which the guide enumerates. There were, for instance, eight tennis clubs in the area of which only three have survived and of these the Lowther Club grounds are much reduced in size. The two cinemas have gone and likewise two places of worship, although Sheen Hall was not then listed. The Ranelagh Club was flourishing with its four polo pavilions, 18 hole golf course, croquet lawns and fashionable club house, and 'The Limes' in Mortlake High Street was still the seat of local government.

The transport information was most comprehensive giving a table of both season ticket and cheap day rates from Barnes and Mortlake to Waterloo. A 3-monthly 3rd class season from the former cost £2.15s.0d., but for the bowler hatted city tycoon £4.2s.6d gave him a first class seat. When the housewives travelled after 9.30 a.m. 1/- return was all that was asked of them and they could return by any train they chose. Alternatively road transport was frequent and varied. There were Nos. 9, 33, 72, 73 buses passing through the Borough all days of the week. In addition the useful 207 provided a circular route to Richmond Park golf course via Priory, Clarence and Roehampton Lanes. Nor were Green Lines lacking, for no less than six routes called at Barnes Red Lion. No public library was listed but mention is made of the Mortlake Parochial Library in Alder Road under an Hon. Librarian, But with rates at 9s.6d. in the £ perhaps a public library was too much to expect. The electricity and gas tariffs fill one with delight. The Borough was proud of its own Electricity Works and, after

a most reasonable fixed charge based on the rateable value of the dwelling, a unit cost a farthing in the summer and a halfpenny in the winter months. With gas supplied for 3s.7½d. 1,000 cubic ft. most residents were well satisfied.

Strangely the guide gives scant attention to the many organisations which flourished at that period. The Barnes Horticultural Society charged a shilling a year for membership, and that included admission to the three annual shows at the Green School. Alas, there was then no History Society.

The street map shows comparatively little change. A few names have been altered e.g. Railway Street, now Westfields Avenue, while Hampton and Columbia Squares together with the West Middlesex Water Works have vanished altogether. The Borough's pride in its Coat of Arms, Mayor, eight Aldermen and twenty-four Councillors was even more short-lived.

The foreword pointed out that "one cannot speak too highly of the advantages to be derived by residents in the Barnes locality…" a well-known physician states that there is "no place that excels it" and "we feel it will then be allowed, without shadow of doubt, that the Borough of Barnes holds a proud place among the environs of the great Metropolis."
And, sentimentally, there may well be some people who will say "Hear, Hear."

Printed May 1978/Newsletter number 65

Right: *Barnes, Mortlake & East Sheen. The Official Guide.* 1st Edition published by The Abbey Publicity Service Ltd. 1937. In the collection of Mr. R. C. Gill

BARNES
MORTLAKE and
EAST SHEEN

NOT · FOR · OURSELVES · ALONE

The

Official Guide

Missing items of Barnes Church Plate

Following the recent discovery[1] at St. Peter's Church, Clapham of a missing brass from St. Mary's Church, Barnes, it seems only appropriate to record the whereabouts of two pieces of plate which are no longer kept in their original surroundings.

In March 1959 an item appeared in a catalogue of Sotheby's described as 'A very fine Edward VI spoon, "knopped with a fluted ball" which shows traces of gilt, the stem engraved "Ad usum Eccles de Berns".' This engraving on the back of the stem is definitely of a later date but the spoon itself was probably made in London 1551. It is interesting to record it fetched £76 when sold in 1959 and is now to be seen in the Assheton-Bennett collection on loan to the Manchester Art Gallery.

The second missing item is recorded in a book on the Church Plate of the Diocese of Landaff (1902). At St. Catherine's Church, Canton, Cardiff, there is a flagon with the inscription "In usum Ecclcsiae de Bernes 1846". It bears the London hallmark for that year and the maker's marks, CTF over GF, agree exactly with a set of Communion Plate at Barnes Parish Church. This information came to light in 1934 and, at that date, contact was made by correspondence with Canon Rees, the incumbent, and also the Rev. J. Baker who was the first Vicar of the parish when it was created in 1894. The latter stated that he understood the flagon had been provided by the Rev. W.E. Rosedale, Rector of St. John's, Cardiff, out of whose large parish St. Catherine's had been created. How this flagon ever reached South Wales has not been ascertained but perhaps some member of the Society would care to do further research and find how it was that two articles of plate should leave the Parish Church during the nineteenth century.

I am greatly indebted to Mr Arthur Grimwade F.S.A., who recently lectured to the Society, in making these notes and correspondence of his freely available and thus adding further knowledge concerning missing property of St. Mary's, Barnes.

Printed May 1975/Newsletter number 53

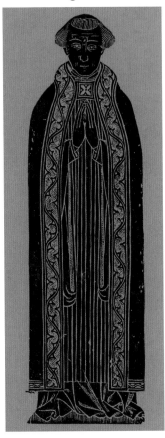

Brass of Nicholas Clerk, Rector of Barnes, died 1480. Originally on the north side of the altar at St Mary's Church, Barnes, this disappeared in the 19th century. Its identity, long unknown, has recently been established by comparison with a rubbing of the Clerk brass

[1] The Clerk Brass was found in St. Peter's Church, Manor Street, Clapham SW4 c.1974. It has been there since 1912 (recorded in a Newsletter article, September 1974 by Raymond Gill).

Barnes flora

Elizabethan Plantsmen

In my January 1993 copy of the *Journal of the Royal Horticultural Society* there is an article on "Elizabethan Plantsmen" by Celia Fisher. These men formed a fraternity of collectors who "throng the pages of Gerard's *Herball*". They created a "network of collectors from Lancashire to Constantinople" and fortunately two interesting plants are recorded as being found in Barnes.

Sir Francis Walsingham had toadflax[1] *(Kickxia spuria)* growing by his house at Barn Elms, while near by "the smallest fluellen grew by the House of Master Bele, chief Clerk to the Queen's Council". This latter gentleman was Robert Beale[2] of Milbourne House. This was quoted by Stephen Bredwell who wrote the dedication to the *Herball* and showed the plants to Gerard.

John Gerard (1545-1612)
From an engraving by John Payne on the title page of the 1633 edition of the *Herball*

Plants are not Gerard's only interest for he also refers to fruit trees in this area: "The greatest variety of rare plums are to be found in the grounds of Master Vincent Pointer of Twickenham". Pointer was also a "most cunning and curious grafter of apples" and planted "all manner of rare fruits". Possibly these 'rare fruits' might be considered quite common today, but it is more likely that the plums and apples grown by Pointer have long vanished and are quite unobtainable.

Printed March 1994/Newsletter number 128

[1] Toadflax is still the common name, but the botanical name is now Linaria Vulgaris.

[2] Sir Robert Beale travelled to Fotheringay Castle with Mary Queen of Scots' death warrant in 1587.

Sir Francis Walsingham

In Memoriam **The Elms of Barnes Churchyard**

Planted   4th February 1652
Felled   7th November 1977

*Lovely and pleasant in their lives
and in their death they were not divided.*

Their ashes are scattered in this churchyard beneath their former shade.

These elms appeared in many prints of St Mary's Church. They were planted by Robert Lenthall, a cousin of William Lenthall, Speaker of the Long Parliament. He described himself as Minister of Barnes and had the care of the parish from 1648-1654. In his own hand on the last page of the 1652 register he wrote the following:-

St Mary's Church, date and artist unknown. This illustration is prior to 1852 by which time the triple lancet windows at the east end had been uncovered and restored. The stage coach ran at frequent intervals from the White Hart on the Terrace to the Strand

"Momorand. Feb.ye 4th 1652 ye 4 elmes and 2 ashes by ye path from the Church gate to ye South porch of ye Parish Church of Barnes, as likewise one ash towards ye east corner of ye Church yarde southward by ye wall nier all seaven of them planted by R. Lenthall then minister of Barnes".

Now these elms have succumbed to Dutch Elm disease and old age, so, after 525 years the appearance of the churchyard is altered. Robert Lenthall planted for posterity. Let us hope his example will be copied in 1978.

The Lobjoits – Market Gardeners of Barnes

For many decades, and especially during the last century, Barnes was renowned for its market gardens. In the early hours of the morning carts set out for Covent Garden while water and even foot transport is recorded as being used. One of the most prosperous of these gardens was undoubtedly the one owned by the Lobjoit family, originally of Huguenot descent.

William John Lobjoit, who began work in Hammersmith, obtained the lease of the east end of the old Workhouse land in 1837 for £75 p.a. He had already been working Harman's field[1] of ten acres for the past four years but this was on the Barn Elms estate and he was not then apparently a resident. His new home was quite extensive stretching from what is now Gipsy Lane to the Putney boundary with Queen's Ride and the Upper Richmond Road to the north and south. He came to Barnes as a young married man with a small son bearing the same name, and a year old daughter Maria, her mother's name-sake. While in Barnes three more children were born and baptized in St. Mary's and later family weddings were solemnized within its walls. William Lobjoit soon identified himself with local affairs. He attended Vestry meetings, paid £15 p.a. for a church pew and in 1839 and 1840 was a Highway Surveyor and an Overseer of the Poor. He increased his land holding on the Workhouse site and in later years his son added extra acreage across the Putney boundary in the Upper Richmond Road.

In 1845 his work was hampered by the laying of the railway line. As he now farmed all the old Workhouse ground he said that "owing to severance there will be difficulty of access for ploughing and dressing; a pale fence at least 5ft high will be required for the protection of fruit and the shade of the fence will injure the available cultivation; fresh paths must be made. One level crossing is desired. Compensation suggested £485.12.6,"
A compromise appears to have been made with the Richmond Railway Co. and a culvert was to be provided by them under the road at the east end of Lobjoit's land.

Lobjoit's farm at Heston

Lobjoit's demise was a tragic accident. He was burnt to death in a Covent Garden Market fire in 1859 and his charred remains lie buried in Old Putney Cemetery on Lower Putney Common, just across from the Barnes/Putney boarder. His business was taken over by his son usually referred to as W.J. He had been married the previous year in St. Mary's Barnes, to Emma Armstrong of Putney. He became a very clever vegetable grower and an astute business man increasing his acreage of market gardens in other Surrey and Middlesex areas. Lobjoit's Green Cos Lettuce reigned supreme for a hundred years and is still listed in many seed catalogues. In August 1860 W.J. left the old Workhouse lands and the Vestry decided to let the farm on building leases. To-day it is covered by houses and large blocks of flats, a very different aspect from the market ground of the last century.

W.J. continued to farm on the land behind Castelnau increasing his holding of Harman's field but finally relinquishing his last Barnes foothold in 1892 when the reservoirs were to be constructed. Sadly about this time two of his sons had died within a year of each other and he left most of his business to his sons

[1] Harman's field, until recently used for allotments, is now beneath the Barnes Waterside development.

William G. and Edward. They undoubtedly flourished for between 1904 and 1920 the Lobjoits had over 1,000 acres under cultivation around London and two stands in Covent Garden. W.J. died in 1925 at the advanced age of eighty-three and four years later his son William (W.G.) was knighted for "services to horticulture".

In 1961, after 125 years, the Covent Garden stand was given up. But even at that date the firm of W.J. Lobjoit & Son Ltd. was still in business[2] at Priory Farm, Burnham, Bucks, with a fifth generation of Lobjoits at work.

Printed May 1975/Newsletter number 53

Material Supplied by:

Barnes Vestry Minutes, St. Mary's Church Registers; Mrs Jessie Lobjoit Collins (grand-daughter of W.J.); *The Grower Magazine*, October 9th 1965; and *The Sunday Times*, March 23rd, 1980.

[2] The last member of the Lobjoit family in farming, Edward Lobjoit, sold up his pig farm near Cullumpton, Devon in 1999.

Wild Flowers

Barnes had wild flowers in great profusion and in *Flora of Surrey*, complied in 1863 by J.A. Brewer there are listed the names of thirteen rare species, some of which he describes as "very copious" or "abundant".

In the summer of 1907 Miss Atwell, a member of the school board, awarded a prize for the largest collection of wild flowers gathered by the girls of Westfields School from the Common and hedgerows. The winner collected 143 varieties, but the total number identified overall was 212.

Printed 1992/Highways and Byways of Barnes

The Acacia Man

A visitor at Barnes Fair introduced himself to the stall helpers of the History Society and spoke to us about the false acacia trees (*Robinia pseudoacacia*) which grow in Queen Elizabeth Walk.

He has since taken his interest further and written to the Forestry Authority at Westonbirt Arboretum giving details of their measurements.

From the reply he received it seems there is little doubt that these trees were planted by William Cobbett, who is described in the letter as 'the acacia man'. Apparently they have grown rather more slowly than one at Kew, but even so their age and size date them as having been planted about 1828 which corresponds with the time Cobbett was farming on the Home Farm at Barn Elms.

Printed 1992 from Highways and Byways of Barnes

These acacias are now protected because of the bats which have taken up residence in them

Local gossip

A Minor Scandal

Mr Arbor-Cooke, now living in Wales, has supplied the Society over a number of years with much detailed information of his family history in connection with their ownership of Milbourne House, Barnes. He has recently sent us some unusual material concerning a case of "wife-bashing" which must have caused raised eyebrows at the time.

In 1692 Sir Miles and Lady Cooke were living in a rented house in Jermyn Street, St James's. Sir Miles was "of Barnes" and certainly owned Milbourne House, which they most likely occupied on occasions. Sir Miles died in 1699 and his widow, Lady Mary Cooke, then went to lodge with Mrs Betts, whose house was probably in the St James's area. She was still residing there when she married Thomas Turner some time after his second wife died on 1 April 1704.

When the marriage took place, Mrs Betts gave up her house and joined the Turners as housekeeper. As a Master-in-Chancery, Turner would have had a town house as well as his estate at Kingston, near Canterbury. It soon became clear that the union was unlikely to last and it was Mrs Betts who was called as chief witness in a court case which ultimately led to the breakdown of the marriage. She stated that Mr Turner treated his wife with great severity and on one occasion threw a brass candlestick at her, kicked her harshly on the leg and generally behaved in such a manner that she did not wish to be alone in a room with him. In the summertime Mr Turner would not allow his wife to accompany him to his country estate in Kent, and by 1708 the marriage had broken down, Mr Turner making no attempt to provide any maintenance for his wife.

Consequently, in that year Mrs Turner, or Lady Cooke as she seems to have preferred being named, came to Barnes, bringing Mrs Betts with her. It is presumed she took up residence in Milbourne House, but as there are no extant rate books of this date it is difficult to be certain. However, Lady Cooke managed to get her own back on Thomas Turner as she refused to return the jewellery which she had received from him and which he complained about in his will. She probably thought this was recompense for his making her no allowance.

Lady Cooke lived to a considerable age; she was baptized in 1648 and her will was said to have been proved in 1731, although it cannot be traced in that year so she may have died earlier. She had actually been married three times, her first husband being a member of the Agar family, also owners of Milbourne House prior to Sir Miles Cooke, so she must have felt some attachment to the house in connection with two of her husbands. It is not known where Lady Cooke was buried or what happened to the faithful Mrs Betts. If she outlived Lady Cooke, it is to be hoped that some provision was made for her in the latter's will.

Printed June 1993/Newsletter number 125

Milbourne House, Barnes

Ghoulies and Ghosties

In the Christmas 1976 edition of the *Barnes & Mortlake Herald* an article appeared on Ghosts in this neighbourhood, but no mention was made of the occult manifestations which are said to have appeared on Barnes Common. Perhaps, as the subject has recently been raised in the local press, this offers a timely opportunity for further information.

This first story I heard related nearly 50 years ago by a gentleman who lived for some years in Putney, and whose parents had spent their lives there. It appears that some time in the 19th century a Putney butcher was discovered one morning, near Barnes Common Cemetery, lying dead in his own blood. It was said that where the blood had lain no grass grew and would not do so until his assassin was found. However, the villain was not discovered and presumably these patches are still bare, though after the great drought of 1976 it would be difficult to identify them today.

In 1932 Mr Elliott O'Donnell published a book entitled *Ghosts of London*. Here in Chapter 16 he relates at some length the story of a ghostly nun appearing to a young man in the vicinity of the cemetery. She was hovering round the place where portions of the body of a certain unfortunate Mrs Thomas had been unearthed. Later the same black robed figure was seen by two members of a family who lived on the outskirts of the common. During the night the nun was observed in the corner of the bedroom of an invalid gentleman, Mr West. His wife could not see her, but his sister-in-law and a maid had observed this phenomenon earlier in the evening in the garden. Mr West persisted in his statement that the woman was staring at him all night and he was "taken so ill that he remained in bed and never left it, for he died the next day".

It will be noticed that both these stories are connected with Barnes Cemetery. It is likely that before lights were placed on the Common paths the railed off area with its white tombstones and dark evergreens must have appeared very eerie on cloudy, moonlight nights.

Printed May 1977/Newsletter number 61

Barnes Old Cemetery, Barnes Common, 1916
The lodge and railings have gone and the cemetery lies vandalised and derelict today

Mumming in Barnes

The following extract is from *Folk-lore in the Home Counties* by T. Fairman Ordish, F.S.A. (1899).

It was my lot a few years ago to witness a very interesting piece of folk-lore in a Surrey district now very closely associated with London. On the evening of November 30th 1891, I walked down the village street of Barnes – it is now the High Street, but new shop fronts cannot even disguise its original character as a typical village street. It was, if I remember rightly, a Saturday night, and a well-known butchery shop in the village was very brilliantly lighted up. Within the circle of illumination there was a small crowd standing in the roadway. In front of these folk and between them and the shop, were some lads and boys in fantastic and quaint attire going through some antics. Happily, I paused to look and listen. In a moment or two I recognised that a traditional folk-play was in course of enactment; the Christmas mumming-play, once a prevalent feature in rural winter activities, still existing here and there in various parts of the country; but here, in Barnes! Yet it was so, and the version of the play was not the most debased or attenuated in my collection. The dresses were mostly very good, and recognizable descendants of types familiar from examples elsewhere in purer form.

The characters were Turkish Knight, St. George, Indian Prince, Father Christmas, Johnny Jack, Doctor and Sweep. A very amusing character was "Johnny Jack" enacted by a small youth with much gusto and a spirited style of declamation. With bent back, and a bunch of undressed wooden dolls tied up on his shoulders, he announced himself - after the traditional manner observed by the characters in all these plays – "Here comes I, little Johnny Jack, with my wife and family on my back". Now that is an incident in the mumming-play which I have not encountered elsewhere, and possibly it may prove to be one of great interest. Such are the pleasant surprises which await the collector of folk-lore. A reference, in the words recited by one of the characters, to "Billy Button from Brentford," confirmed what I ascertained otherwise, that this "cry of players" came from the other side of the river, as they and others of previous generations had been accustomed to do, time out of mind. The sudden appearance of these figures in their quaint and fantastic costumes beneath the brilliant lights of the butcher's shop, as I emerged from the darkness, made a vivid impression on my memory, and I thus secured most unexpectedly an additional item for my collection of English Folk-drama.

Printed May 1975/Newsletter number 53

The butcher's shop was in all likelihood that of Seal's. Being close to Stanton Road there would have been extra space in the roadway

… a well-known butchery shop in the village was very brilliantly lighted up. Within the circle of illumination there was a small crowd standing in the roadway. In front of these folk and between them and the shop, were some lads and boys in fantastic and quaint attire going through some antics

Barnes memories

Water Rat Cottage

Intermittently during the 1950s the *Barnes and Mortlake Herald* published reminiscences and illustrations sent in by elderly readers recalling childhood memories.

Among the contributors was Mr John Ellis who persuaded his 84-year-old great-aunt to tell him about her Barnes childhood. She was born in 1870 in Beverley Cottage which stood in Station Road between Creek Bridge and Beverley Road. She described it as a long, wooden bungalow-style building with a large fruit orchard at the back which ran nearly the length of Beverley Road. When these premises were sold for housing development, her father, known as 'Paddy' Ellis, moved to Water Rat Cottage. This stood at the end of the present Willow Avenue, near the gates of Beverley Works, and he renamed their new home Beverley Cottage after their previous dwelling. The houses erected in Station Road on the site of their old home were known as Carlton Terrace, and were themselves demolished about 1962 to make way for the new police station.

Printed June 1992/Newsletter number 121

Childhood Memories

The Rev. B. Copleston, Rector of Barnes (1859-1865) was the father of two Bishops in India. From time to time, when on furlough, they revisited and preached in their birth-place.

On September 3rd 1905, the Bishop of Calcutta, Metropolitan and Primate of All India, addressed the local children in St. Michael's Church. He said there was something about Barnes boys and girls that he had a particular love for, because he was a Barnes boy himself. He had played on the Green, taken slides on the Pond, and caught eels in the Beverley Brook. But the greatest pleasure he looked back upon was when all the children came to the Rectory to play on the occasion of a great parish festival.

It would be interesting to learn whether any of our residents have caught fish in Beverley Brook and if so of what species and how recently.

Printed June 1992/Newsletter number 121

He had played on the Green, taken slides on the Pond, and caught eels in the Beverley Brook.

Sir Arthur Bliss
Childhood Memories of Barnes and Mortlake

Barnes has been fortunate in the number of musicians and composers that at various times have lived within its environs. Gustav Holst resided on Barnes Terrace and wrote music for the school kept by his aunt, Mrs. Newman. Herbert Howells dwelt for many years in Beverley Close and in Arthur Bliss's autobiography *As I Remember* there are delightful references to his childhood spent overlooking Barnes Common.

He was born in 1891 in Hawthornden in Queen's Ride. The house, which was destroyed in World War II, was so named because of the deep red variety of hawthorn bushes that grew in the circular drive up to the front door of the house. One of his earliest memories is that of a fire on the Common opposite. The gorse bushes had caught alight and the flames spread rapidly in a strong wind. He recalls how, awakened by shouts, he went to his bedroom window and watched "with frightened fascination dark shapes leaping around with brooms as they beat out the flames which had rapidly approached our road." Occasionally a Sunday treat was to drive over to Mortlake with his father and brothers to have tea with his grandmother. One of the pleasures afforded by these visits, apart from delicious cakes, was that her garden ran down to the river and this was especially favoured on Boat Race days. He even faithfully records how disks of either light or dark blue paper floated over the garden to record the winner of the event.

Also living in the Mortlake house was his Uncle Kennard who had retired there after working, for many years, in China. He gave the Bliss boys a Chinese vase as a present. It was about two feet high with a lid and a key in its side. On being wound up music could be heard from within, the lid slowly opened and "a Mandarin in green silk with long drooping moustaches" slowly rose up and held a cup of tea to his lips. After "more salutations in which his long moustaches quivered he would gracefully withdraw and the lid would close over him." Unfortunately there is no further reference to this enchanting vase and one wonders if it still exists today.

Sadly Bliss's mother died in 1895 and the family moved to Holland Park, Bayswater. Sometime after his death his ashes were buried in Mortlake Cemetry, South Worple Way, in proximity to the graves of other family members.

Printed September/Newsletter number 154

Bliss's headstone in Mortlake Cemetery

Calling All Parents

During the 1950s a very lively organisation flourished in the one-time borough of Barnes under the title of the Barnes Parents' Association. It had as its aims a number of promotions which were intended to further the interest and welfare of parents and children.

To this end such concerns as local education, road safety, pram ramps, maternity and child welfare, and children's recreation centres were kept to the forefront by lectures and discussions to encourage co-operation between local government, schools and home. The minimum subscription of 1s (5p) per annum entitled members to attend meetings and take part in social activities. These included picnics in Richmond Park, sports on Palewell Common and swimming galas in Richmond Baths. But this energetic group extended its influence outside the locality as it was instrumental in starting the popular radio programme for under five year olds, namely "Listen with Mother."

In order to remain solvent, an annual pantomime was produced at the now demolished Wigan Hall in North Worple Way, Mortlake. This ran for several nights and was extremely popular. In 1955 "Dick Whittington", written by Cllr F.A.W. Counter, was acclaimed in the *Barnes Herald* as a "Big Success" and four columns of print and a photograph of the cast were in the issue of 11 February. This was followed in 1956 with "Aladdin and his Wonderful Lamp", in 1957 with "Puss in Boots", "Cinderella" in 1958 and the last one in 1959. This was "Robinson Crusoe" written by two of the members, Cllr Counter and Mr F.J. Norris. Six performances were given of this production from 17-24 January and a photograph of the Principal Boy, Mrs Mary Hovenden, with her three young daughters appeared in the *Evening News* for 21 January, so fame had extended beyond the parish boundaries. As one who attended these productions there are memories of outstanding costumes, clever home-produced scenery and much versatility among those taking part. Children danced, conjurors mystified and local jokes abounded. The rehearsals took place on

Sunday afternoons and one long-suffering father, left in charge of his youngsters, was reported to have said, when attending a performance, that all the Sunday dinner washing-up had been worth it after all.

In the 1960s the Association was wound up as by then Parent-Teacher Associations were formed in schools and the old Borough of Barnes was swallowed up by the Greater London Borough of Richmond upon Thames. Also the infants and toddlers of the original members were by then past their childhood years and there was no longer the incentive to keep going. I am most indebted to former members for providing so much information. These include Mrs Mary Hovenden for lending me original programmes, photographs and newspaper cuttings, Mrs Eileen Keogh for showing me hers and filling in gaps with personal reminiscences, and Mrs Barbara Andrew with her amusing memories of swimming galas and sports days.

Printed December 1998/Newsletter number 147

… one long-suffering father, left in charge of his youngsters, was reported to have said, when attending a performance, that all the Sunday dinner washing-up had been worth it after all.

Bus Journeys from Barnes to Hammersmith before World War II

When my parents married in 1907 they came to live in Barnes and one reason for this choice was that there was a motor bus service to Hammersmith.

True, my father would recall frequent breakdowns en route but apparently the passengers alighted and boarded the next bus which came along soon after. My personal memories really begin in the 1920s when I travelled daily to school in Brook Green, Hammersmith. At that time buses stopped on request anywhere along the route. It was only necessary to hold up your hand, and conversely you rang the bell once to stop the bus wherever you wished to alight. There were official fare stages and those from the garage to Hammersmith were Avondale Road, Sun Inn, Red Lion. Boileau Arms and Hammersmith Broadway. The fare was 1d for two stages, i.e. Sun Inn to Boileau Arms, Red Lion to Hammersmith, etc. Children under 14 were half price so that for a number of years I only paid 1d from the Sun Inn to Rowan Road, across Hammersmith Broadway. I still have a ticket in my scrapbook. It is made of thin card and measures 1½ x 2¼ inches. All the fare stages are printed opposite each other and the conductor punched the place you boarded and this showed you where to alight. 1d tickets were white, 2d blue, 3d

This 46 seat, K type motor bus (1919-1932), is the same type as the one I would have travelled on

pink and 4d green. There were others but I seldom used them. The 6d were a muddy chocolate colour but I cannot recall what a 5d was like.

One of my 1d, Route 9 tickets, showing both sides – this one was found in a school text book and used as a bookmarker.

For a number of my school years the buses were uncovered on top and unheated inside. We clambered up exposed stairs from the conductor's platform and sat on slatted wooden seats with wooden backs. These had a weatherproof cover ("apron", I think, was its technical name) and on wet days passengers huddled under one and kept the rain off their laps. The disadvantage was that when you got up the rainwater was liable to go down the back of the people seated in front of you. In the front of the bus, above the driver, was a wooden board which stated the destination. It fitted into two metal slots, one at each end. It was the delight of Colet Court boys to reverse these boards, upside down was even better, but conductors were alert to these pranks and threatened to turn the culprits off.

In the late 1920s and early 1930s what were known as "Pirate" buses appeared on the road. These were owned by small private companies or even individuals and they rushed along at speed, hoping to arrive at a stop before the London General and pick up waiting passengers. One particular friend of mine and I would board different buses, go on top, and wave to each other as the vehicles passed and re-passed each other along Castelnau. Needless to say whoever won waited for the loser on arriving at our destination. The conductors from Mortlake garage were a friendly body of men. We all recognised each other and in some cases father and son worked on the same bus as driver and conductor. Help was given to people boarding and alighting, especially the elderly or mothers with small children. No more than five people were allowed to stand inside and none on the top deck. In the rush hour a careful count was made of vacant seats and only the requisite number of passengers were allowed on. When the bus had a full load the conductor rang the bell three times and the driver would not stop at requests along the route.

But even in those days we experienced delays. In the 1920s Castelnau and Church Road had a wooden road surface. After heavy rain these blocks would swell and push upwards thus making the road impassable. Then there were diversions round side turnings and lengthy hold-ups. This was all controlled by local police – no automatic signals then – but the volume of traffic was still light and horse-drawn vehicles were a common sight.

It interests me now to realise that when I took for granted a motor bus for my school journey there must have been many Barnes residents who could recall that 20 years before they had only seen horse-drawn ones.

Printed September 1996/Newsletter number 138

This ticket's reverse shows that on a Sunday it was possible to travel beyond Liverpool Street, as far as Dalston

These so-called "geographical" bell punch tickets, naming all the stages on each route on every ticket, remained in use until March 1952. They were replaced by "deaf and dumb" tickets showing only numbered stages and thereby not specific to particular routes. Mortlake used these tickets until October 1957

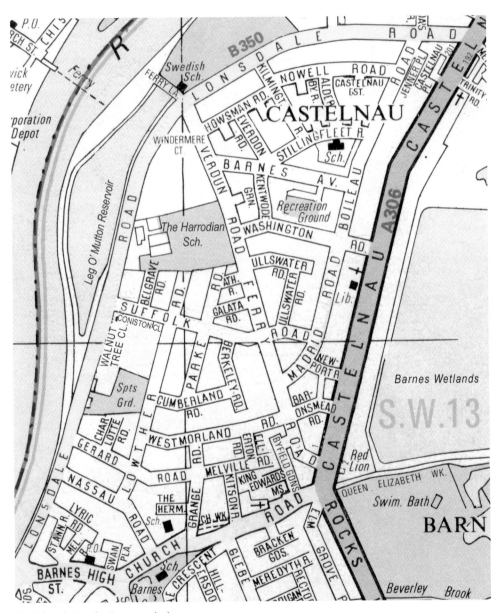

This is how the Lowther Estate now looks.
(Look at this with reference to the facing article.)

Let us now praise famous men

The Lowther family's Suffolk home

Campsea Ashe. I had long had an intention to visit this Suffolk village and when in August last I passed a sign-post indicating it was three miles along a country lane I had no difficulty in suggesting to my host, himself a former Barnes resident, that we make a detour to this village. Apart from this intriguing name it was the place to which the Lowther family moved when St. Ann's, their former Barnes residence, was sold.

The churchyard was the first reward. East of the south porch, along the path, is a plot containing eleven Lowther graves. The eldest member lying here is the Hon. William Lowther and his wife Alice, daughter of Lord Wensleydale. They are surrounded by sons, grandsons and a great grandson, many of them with their wives. Here in this remote country churchyard lies buried James William Lowther, 1st Viscount Ullswater of Campsea Ashe and speaker of the House of Commons from 1905 to 1921. Beside him is his brother the Rt. Hon. Gerard Lowther, G.C. M.G. C.B. P.C., ambassador in Constantinople, and whose other places of official residence have given their names to many Barnes roads. The youngest member of the family died on active service in World War II and his wife three years later.

The interior of the church was also full of Lowther interest. The east window had been erected to the first named couple "by their loving children" and on the south wall of the nave was a mural tablet to Major General Sir Henry Lowther K.C.M.G. C.B. C.M.G. C.V.O. D.S.O. Scots Guards. He, too, was a brother to James and Gerard but not interred with them in the churchyard. The next move was to find the site of the now demolished High House. This was not difficult but sadly its extensive grounds lie ravaged by time and neglect. When the Hon. William bought it in 1883 the whole estate was about four thousand acres and its chief features were the fine cedars and remarkable yew hedges. The

St. Ann's – the family's former Barnes home in 1898.

statuary from St. Ann's was moved here and a small Japanese garden laid out with "a tea-house and tiny lawn with a Japanese well and stepping stones sunk in the grass as required by the custom of the Far East". This was the result of the Hon. Gerard's stay in Tokyo. Now in 1985 these delights can no longer be seen but I felt I had followed the Lowther family, who have left many records of themselves on the Lowther estate in Barnes, to their final resting place.

Printed March 1986/Newsletter number 96

Books of further reference

Suffolk by Augustine Page 1847.
East Suffolk. Illustrated by H.R.Barker 1908-1909;
Country Life, Vol.XVIII, July 15th 1905. This article has twelve photographs of the house and grounds.
A Speaker's Commentaries by Rt.Hon.James William Lowther, Viscount Ullswater G.C.B. LLD DCL, Speaker of the House of Commons 1905-1921. Published in 1925 by Edward Arnold & Co.

A Distinguished Friendship

Dr Robert Willis lived at the Homestead, Church Road, Barnes, from 1845 to 1878. He had been in a local partnership with a former resident there, Dr Scott, and after the latter moved to a West End address, Dr Willis resided in the house. By this time he had already had a varied career.

Having graduated M.D. at Edinburgh University he came south and by 1857 added M.R.C.S. England and L.R.C.P. after his name. In addition he served as Librarian of the Royal College of Surgeons for eighteen years prior to 1845 and had found time for continental travel. Nor was this all for his linguistic achievements were notable, translating important medical works from German, Latin and French into English. He had lectured at the Aldersgate School of Medicine and collaborated with Professor Marks of Göttingen on a book entitled *The Decrease of Disease by Civilisation*. Even by modern standards Dr Willis was a man of great energy.

He had his domestic interest also. He was an ardent gardener and an expert on the budding of roses. Miss Attwell recalls how this tall white-haired Scotsman took her into the Homestead garden and picked her a ripe peach. He had a family of one son and six daughters. Two unmarried girls lived at the Homestead and Miss Attwell considered them both clever and accomplished. The elder painted and Miss Buddy, the younger, had a very beautiful voice. Two others married local doctors who were beloved by Barnes and Mortlake residents. One, Dr William Marshall lived for many years at Torrieburn, the tall house next door to St. Osmunds School and the other, Dr Robert Dunbar Mackintosh, at Marsham Lodge, Mortlake. This site next to the White Hart Hotel is now a block of flats.

But Robert Willis had also a gift for music and this brought him into a close friendship with Benjamin Ward Richardson. He had offered this young man an assistantship in what he described as "one of the best practices in the United Kingdom and in the very cream of British Society". Richardson would find "many who were far more than mere patients", and Willis went on to list Mr E. Cooke R.A., the famous artist, Mr Dawson Turner the antiquarian, Sir Launcelot Shadwell, Vice Chancellor of England, Professor Owen and Sir James Knight-Bruce. In addition Richardson met many leaders of his profession. In his Mortlake residence[1], with the church clock as his timepiece, Richardson fitted up a small laboratory. There were shelves for bottles of specimens and chemicals, physical and chemical apparatus, an old electric battery which Benjamin Franklin had once used and a good microscope. Dr Willis called this room 'The Life Shop' and after a day's work was done he would come there to watch Richardson's experiments and lend a hand. Here they were often joined by other friendly practitioners from the neighbourhood. Richardson found time while at Mortlake for other activities. He read for his degree at

Sir Benjamin Ward Richardson 1828-1896

St. Andrew's, visited London hospitals and studied French and German. He recorded the effect of rowing upon health presumably because his house overlooked the Thames.

In 1855 with the help of three acquaintances he founded the East Surrey Cholera Society. Willis was elected President and meetings were held at Waterloo Hospital for Children. Richardson was already on the Committee of Enquiry appointed by the Mortlake Vestry to deal with the cholera outbreak in this area.

Through Richardson's musical interests he became integrated into the local circle and used to visit Dr Sterndale Bennett, for whose metronome he devised an electric measure. One of Dr Bennett's pupils was Mary Smith of Mortlake. She accompanied Richardson's singing and they courted on Barnes Common prior to announcing their engagement. Richardson was on good terms with the gypsies who encamped there. His first case among them was a boy whose spine had been accidentally broken and often, without fee, he attended at confinements. His mid-wifery experiences led him to write a paper on *The Diseases of the Child Before Birth* which won him the Fothergillian Prize.

In 1854, having obtained his M.D. Richardson set up on his own as a West End physician and three years later married Mary Smith. The couple appear to have retained their interest in this area, probably to visit Mary's family and their many local friends. There is a tombstone in Mortlake Cemetery to their young son Kenneth Benjamin who died 5th October 1864, aged 5 years 10 months. Richardson's friendship with Robert Willis continued until Willis died in 1878 when Richardson wrote in his obituary that he was "one of the lights of this little earth."

Three years before the close of Richardson's very distinguished career he was knighted. His death occurred in 1896, aged 68 years.

Printed December 1978/Newsletter number 67

[1] Richardson's Mortlake residence was at 101, Morlake High Street. This is still standing, but is much altered

Bibliography

Dictionary of National Biography.
Sir Benjamin Ward Richardson by Sir Arthur MacNally. Miss Attwell M.S.
Vita Medica by Benjamin Ward Richardson.
Life of Sir Benjamin Ward Richardson by his daughter.
Times Obituary Notices.
Nineteenth Century Mortlake and East Sheen by C. Marshall Rose.

Old Nassaurians

Local residents may have had Nassau House School brought to their notice for the first time in the Society's publication *Childhood Memories of Barnes Village.* Regretfully Mary Attwell, the headmaster's daughter, does not give a detailed account of the daily life of the school but the book illustrations show groups of the 43 boys in a variety of poses which give some clue to the friendly atmosphere that seems to have contributed to the individual teaching which produced outstanding results.

Many of the most distinguished pupils acknowledged their debt to Professor Attwell's meticulous teaching. Sir Leslie Ward of Spy cartoon fame went there as an eight-year-old and in his biography *Forty Years of Spy* wrote, "Among those still living at an advanced age I am glad to reckon Mrs Attwell, the widow of my old schoolmaster, Professor Attwell; and I take this opportunity to express my deep regard for both of them,

and appreciation of the happy time I spent at their school, Nassau House, Barnes." Further on he refers to Alban Doran, "one of my school fellows (son of my father's friend Dr Doran) who spent his time searching for animalculae or bottling strange insects." Alban Doran was two years older than Leslie Ward and his early interest in scientific subjects – perhaps he fished in Barnes Pond – led him to a distinguished medical career at

St Bartholomew's Hospital. From 1899-1900 he was President of The Obstetrical Society of London.

Another distinguished medical man was Maurice Anderson, whose name is listed as being in Form D in the 1872 record. He went on to University College, London, where he added MB, BS and MRCS after his name. Other honours followed with an MVO in 1906, a knighthood in 1912 and CVO in 1925. In addition he was created a Knight of the Order of St John of Jerusalem and found time to act as a representative on wildlife conservation for The National Trust and to serve on the Executive Committee of the Council for the Preservation of Rural England. Surely a busy and fulfilled life. Other old pupils had distinguished army careers. Brigadier General Robert William Ronaldson entered the army in 1886 and rose rapidly in the ranks. He served in India, South Africa and the First World War, in which he was severely wounded. He retired in 1920, living for another 26 years. General Sir John Asser, three years younger than Ronaldson, also served with great distinction, being awarded an array of medals and a knighthood. He finally retired in 1930. In Form A in 1872 appears the name T.G. Horridge. Fifteen-year-old Thomas Gardner Horridge was not destined to have his name permanently at the bottom of a list. At the age of 22 he was admitted a solicitor and rose to become a judge. In 1906 he was MP for East Manchester and in 1910 was knighted. In 1937, a year before his death, he became a Privy Councillor.

Professor Henry Attwell
in the garden of Nassau House c.1860

Nassau House School[1] ran for the comparatively short time of 30 years. The numbers were never large, probably between 30-40 pupils at any one time, but the classes were small and the boys appear to have come from supportive and intellectual home back-grounds. Yet, with no entrance examination, the future careers of the pupils were of concern to those in whose care they were placed and it appears obvious that the excellent basic groundwork they received repaid teacher and scholar alike.

Printed March 1997/Newsletter number 140

[1] Nassau House, formerly Fern Lodge, stood on the eastern corner of Nassau Road facing Barnes Green. When Henry Attwell closed his school in 1889 he replaced the house with nos. 31-37 Church Road – known to locals as 'Attwell's Folly' as they had basements liable to flood.

Nassau School – 1st Class 1872, second term

The Nassau School Roll,

FOR THE FIRST TERM, 1872.

A

Henry Newton Stevens. *Captain.*
G. Russell.
B. L. Johnson.
T. S. Tetley.
F. Rushworth.
T. G. Horridge.

———

B

H. R. Travis.
E. B. Pyman.
O. J. Rumsey.
J. Eldridge.
N. Rushworth.
W. R. Ward.
W. Cox.
A. Pullman.
G. Shute.
J. H. A. Anderson.
J F Jackson.
P. S. Court.

———

C

W. Burdekin.
F. J. Nesbitt.
J. R. E. Russell.
R. H. Russell.
J. Adams.
F. W. Broadbent.
G. C. Penney.
G. G. Flint.
J. D. Menzies.
A. J. Stokes.
T. S. Walker.
G. Way.
W B. Grove.

———

D

C. D. Gairdner.
W. Andrew.
W. M. A. Anderson.
Raoul de Bourbel.
G. P. Russell.
J. P. Wedgwood.
W. R. Tuxford.
R. J. Money.
A. J. Russell.
H. D. Littlewood.
R. Oldershaw.
A. W. Keith.

Map Index

Numbers on the map locate each article and relate to the
page number within the book

First & Second Wartime Life
Childhood Memories of Barnes in the Great War   7
Christmastide in World War Two (Kitson Rd)   9
Wartime Schooling 1939-1940   12

Peace time emergencies
Fire...Fire! (Red Lion Pub, Castelnau))   15
The great fire at Barn Elms Farm   17
A Christmas Hero (St. Michael's Church Hall)   18
The Great Barnes Flood (Station Rd)   19

Barnes Terrace
The Papendiek Family in Barnes (3 The Terrace)   21
Nurserymen and artists (Elm Bank Gardens)   23
Riverside Delights (9 The Terrace)   24

Lesser Barnes authors
Little-known Barnes writers (Church Rd)   27
Joseph Comyns Carr (Queens Ride)   28
A prolific writer (Scarth Rd)   29
Horse dealing in Barnes (Station Rd)   30

Local Eccentrics
An Eccentric Barnes Farmer (Barn Elms Reservoirs) 31
Old Parr (1 Church Road)   32
Old Reuben (66 Railway St – now Westfields Ave)   33
Hermitage Cottage and Monk Lewis (off Grange Rd)   34
The Arab boy (Millhill)   35
Philip de Waal (Church Rd)   35ᵃ

Parish and people
A Kindly Act (Church Rd)   38
Memories of Essex House (Station Rd)   42
Barnes and Mortlake en Fete (Olympic Studios)   44
Not For Ourselves Alone
(The Limes, 123 Mortlake High St)   46

Barnes flora
Elizabethan Plantsmen (Barn Elms House)   49
The Elms of Barnes Churchyard (St Mary's, Church Rd) 50
The Lobjoits – Market Gardeners of Barnes
(Harman's Field)   51
The Acacia Man (Queen Elizabeth Walk)   52

Local gossip
A Minor Scandal (Milbourne House, Station Rd)   53
Ghoulies and Ghosties (Barnes Cemetery)   54
Mumming in Barnes (Barnes High Street)   55

Barnes memories
Water Rat Cottage (Willow Ave)   57
Sir Arthur Bliss (Queens Ride)   58

Let us now praise famous men
The Lowther family's Suffolk home
(St Ann's House, Lonsdale Rd)   63
A Distinguished Friendship
(The Homestead, Church Rd)   64
(101 Mortlake High St)   64ᵃ
Old Nassaurians (Nassaur Rd)   65